The Prestige Series
Tyne-Tees-Mersey

A Survey of the Limited Stop Pool Services in the North of England 1929 to 1975

Keith Healey and

Philip Battersby

Cover: The principal changing and connecting point for the Tyne-Tees-Mersey services was the coach station at Wellington Street, Leeds. On a quiet day in the mid-1960s an impressive Lancashire United AEC prepared to depart for Liverpool on the X97 via Altrincham, with Ribble and West Yorkshire vehicles in the background. The Plaxton coach body fitted to **91 (615WTE)** of 1962 owed more to the manufacturer's service bus designs than might have been expected. *(Photobus)*

Title page: In a scene at Wellington Street circa 1954, the large, clear and informative destination blinds used by United gave a thumbnail sketch of much of the activity of the Limited Stop Pool. The nearer coach conveyed something of the local service work done in the rural North Riding, whilst the other referred to the large cities which made the Pool services so frequent and lucrative. The vehicles were **BBE18** and **8 (NHN152** and **137)** in United's second BBE class, based on the Bristol LL6B chassis. *(Roy Marshall)*

Opposite page: In the postwar years of peak demand, and before the advent of single-deckers seating 50 and more, the Traffic Commissioners licensed double-deck duplication on the Liverpool - Manchester section. At Lower Mosley Street, Manchester, on 24th September 1955, an inspector was preparing to send Lancashire United's **92 (ETE894)** to Liverpool on such a working. It was not until the late 1960s that similar working was permitted between Manchester and Leeds. The bus shown was a 1940 Leyland TD5 with Weymann lowbridge body equipped with stencil destination indicator. *(W Ryan)*

Rear cover: The Pool timetable leaflets varied in design over the years, and this one was current in the 1950s. The production was handled by West Yorkshire, and the coach sketched by the artist bore a noticeable resemblance to that company's Bristol L6G type of 1939. At this period the word "Express" was used in preference to "Limited Stop", but the compiler did not quite succeed in getting the telephones in numerical order!

Below: The demand for coach travel to holiday destinations in the early postwar years is well illustrated by this 1948 picture of a Sunday morning queue in Feethams, Darlington. The stop sign indicated services to Coventry, Hull, Leeds, Liverpool and London, but coaches for Blackpool and for Great Yarmouth also picked up here. *(C F Klapper)*

LIVERPOOL

92

ETE 894

Operated **TYNE** LIMITED **TEES** *Jointly by*

SERVICES

NORTHERN STOP **UNITED**
General Transport Co. Ltd MERSEY Automobile Services Ltd.

YORKSHIRE **WEST YORKSHIRE**
Woollen District Transport Co. Ltd Road Car Co. Ltd.

NORTH WESTERN **LANCASHIRE UNITED**
Road Car Co. Ltd Transport and Power Co Ltd

Table of Contents

1. Introduction

The "Limited Stop Pool" was a group of bus companies operating joint long distance services linking Liverpool, Manchester and Leeds with Middlesbrough and Newcastle. This survey presents an illustrated history of these operations from their inception in 1929 to their absorption into the National Travel express network in 1973 and the abandonment in 1975 of the licensing of the services to the individual operators. "Limited Stop" indicated that for the most part they provided long distance express services rather than local stopping services, and "Pool" indicated that the expenses and receipts were pooled and shared out according to an agreed formula.

The Pool and its services were universally known as "The Limited Stop", and the name appeared in timetables, on tickets and on destination blinds. The term "Northern Pool" was also used, but mainly on reports by secretaries of companies from 1937 onwards. This gave the title an air of being official, but it was not in popular use either outside or within the bus industry. The service was also widely

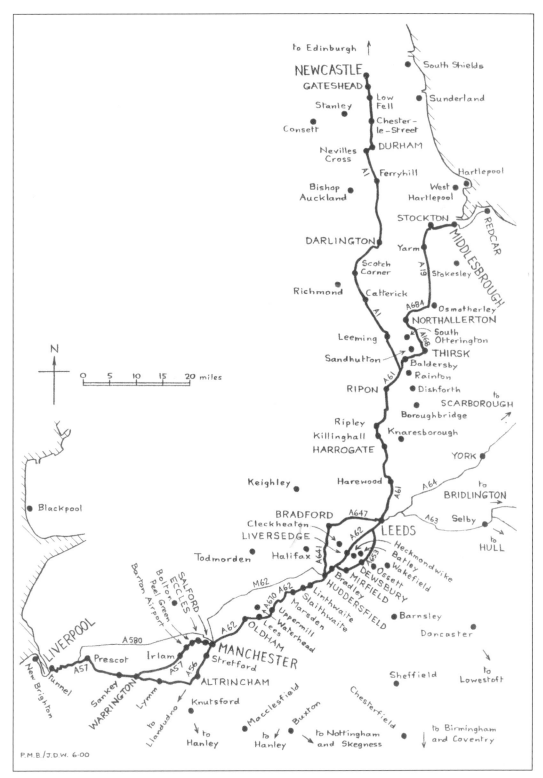

This map shows the principal services of the Limited Stop Pool and the appropriate Ministry of Transport road numbers. Thick lines represent the basic all-year services in the lengthy stable period of the Pool's history. Thin lines depict sections that were seasonal or short-lived. Places reached by connecting services, even where these were licensed to all the Pool operators, are indicated by dots or arrows, as are most of the other places mentioned in the text.

referred to as "Tyne-Tees-Mersey" in the postwar period. This was a publicity slogan rather than a title, and survived for a while with National Travel after the "Limited Stop" name had gone. Postwar publicity also featured the Pool's own symbol, which was an inverted triangle containing a circle.

For most of its history, the six Pool operators were:-

NORTH WESTERN Road Car Company Ltd, Stockport,
NORTHERN General Transport Company Ltd, Gateshead,
WEST YORKSHIRE Road Car Company Ltd, Harrogate,
YORKSHIRE Woollen District Transport Company Ltd, Dewsbury,
LANCASHIRE UNITED Transport Ltd, Atherton and
UNITED Automobile Services Ltd, Darlington.

In the early years two other companies were involved:-

CROSVILLE Motor Services Ltd, Chester and
EAST YORKSHIRE Motor Services Ltd, Hull.

Two further companies were Pool members in the final years:-

HEBBLE Motor Services Ltd, Halifax, replacing Yorkshire Woollen District, and
RIBBLE Motor Services Ltd, Preston, replacing Lancashire United.

The United head office was at York when the company was first discussing its possible Pool membership, but moved to Darlington at the beginning of 1932. Several changes to company names occurred in both the early and the later years. The Crosville Motor Company Ltd adopted the 'Services' form in 1930, and the Yorkshire (Woollen District) Electric Tramways Company Ltd took the wider 'Transport' title in 1935 after the abandonment of its tramways. On the other hand, a more restricted name was assumed by Lancashire United in 1948 when 'and Power Company' was dropped from the title after the electricity side of the undertaking was nationalised. In 1974 Hebble was renamed **NATIONAL TRAVEL (NORTH EAST)** Ltd, and North Western became **NATIONAL**

TRAVEL (NORTH WEST) Ltd, reflecting their new status as coach operators within the National Bus Company. Throughout this survey, the operators will be referred to in their usual colloquial forms, particularly 'Northern' and 'United', rather than in the fuller forms which the trade press often preferred. The exceptions are Yorkshire Woollen District, denoted here as 'Yorkshire WD', and Lancashire United, sometimes shown as 'LUT' in accordance with its own practice.

After the passing of the Road Traffic Act 1930, the Pool companies had to deal with the Traffic Commissioners of three different Traffic Areas. These were designated North Western, Yorkshire and Northern. To prevent possible confusion between the Traffic Areas and similarly named bus operators, the former will be referred to as the North Western TA, Yorkshire TA and Northern TA throughout. Similarly, the letters TC will denote the Traffic Commissioners of those Areas. Other abbreviations will in customary form describe the days of the week (SuMTuWThFS), with BH for Bank Holidays and O for Only. Money is referred to in the forms that were current at the time, with the abbreviations 's' for shilling and 'd' for pence. Twenty shillings (20s) = one pound (£1), and one shilling (1s) = 12 pence (12d) = 5 new pence (5p). The decimal currency was introduced on 15th February 1971.

In the text, the place name 'Newcastle' refers in every instance to Newcastle upon Tyne. The occasional reference to Newcastle in Staffordshire will be in the form 'Newcastle-under-Lyme'. A particular difficulty occurs in describing the Tees-side section, which operated to Redcar in prewar summers, but otherwise only as far as Middlesbrough. In most circumstances, such terms as 'Middlesbrough section' and 'Redcar section' should be regarded as synonymous, except where differences are specified.

It will be readily apparent that this is the story of the services operated by the Limited Stop Pool, not a book about the vehicles used on those services. However, in the cases of Tyne & Mersey, Overland and Fawdon there is some description of their fleets. The reason for their inclusion is that this information has not so far been published anywhere else. In particular, the lists of former vehicles of acquired operators in the Northern and West Yorkshire fleet histories make no mention of them. We hope that readers will not feel that an imbalance is created by the inclusion of this detail here.

Upon the introduction of the services from Manchester to Hull, Scarborough and Bridlington on 6th July 1929 the four original Limited Stop operators were joined by East Yorkshire and issued these timetable leaflets. Note that the Hull and Bridlington services operated via Selby. When these journeys were finally withdrawn in 1934, passengers east of Leeds could use the joint East Yorkshire and West Yorkshire stage carriage services instead, but they took the longer route via York.

SERVICE No. 61 Cont.—Manchester, Oldham, Huddersfield, Leeds, Harrogate, Darlington, Newcastle-on-Tyne.
(Shewing connections at Manchester to and from Liverpool.)

Operated jointly by North Western Road Car Co. Ltd., Northern General Transport Co. Ltd., Yorkshire (W.D.)
Electric Tramways, Ltd. and West Yorkshire Road Car Co. Ltd.

Week-days and Sundays.

		am	am	am	am	am	pm	pm	pm	pm	pm
Newcastle (Worswick Street)	dep.			6 25	8*25	10*25	12 25	2 25	4 25	6 25	8 25
Durham (Omnibus Station)	,,			7 10	9 10	11 10	1 10	3 10	5 10	7 10	9 10
Darlington (Lead Yard)	,,			8 0	10 0	12 0	2 0	4 0	6 0	8 0	10 0
Catterick (County Hotel)	arr.			8 40	10 40	12 40	2 40	4 40	6 40	8 40	10 40
	dep.			9 0	11 0	1 0	3 0	5 0	7 0	9 0	10 50
Ripon (Market Place)	,,			9 50	11 50	1 50	3 50	5 50	7 50	9 50	11 40
Harrogate (Low Harrogate Booking Office)	,,		8 40	10 25	12 25	2 25	4 25	6 25	8 25	10 25	12 15
Harewood (Harewood Arms)	,,		9 5	10 50	12 50	2 50	4 50	6 50	8 50	10 50	
Leeds (Wellington St. 'Bus Station)	arr.		9 30	11 15	1 15	3 15	5 15	7 15	9 15	11 15	
	dep.	7 35	9 35	11 35	1 35	3 35	5 35	7 35	9 35	11 20	
Liversedge (Swan Hotel)	,,	8 0	10 0	12 0	2 0	4 0	6 0	8 0	10 0	11 55	
Huddersfield (Kirkgate)	,,	8 20	10 20	12 20	2 20	4 20	6 20	8 20	10 20	12 15	
Marsden (Tram Terminus)	,,	8 45	10 45	12 45	2 45	4 45	6 45	8 45	10 45		
Uppermill (Commercial Hotel)	,,	9 5	11 5	1 5	3 5	5 5	7 5	9 5	11 5		
Oldham (Greaves St. G.P.O.)	,,	9 25	11 25	1 25	3 25	5 25	7 25	9 25	11 25		
Manchester (Lower Mosley St.)	arr.	9 50	11 50	1 50	3 50	5 50	7 50	9 50	11 50		
Liverpool (Mount Pleasant)	arr.	11 55	1 55		5 55	7 55	9 55	11 55			

*—Denotes through journey to and from Liverpool.

Note.—Passengers may break their journey at any of the above points, on day of travel only.

For additional journeys between Manchester and Leeds, see page 13.

LIMITED STOP SERVICE.

**SERVICE No. 61a.—Manchester, Oldham, Huddersfield, Leeds, Selby, Hull,
Bridlington, York and Scarborough.**
(Shewing connections at Manchester to and from Liverpool.)

Operated jointly by East Yorkshire Motor Services Ltd., North Western Road Car Co.,
Ltd., Yorkshire (W.D.) Electric Tramways, Ltd. and West Yorkshire Road Car Co. Ltd.

Week-days and Sundays.

		am	am	am	pm	pm	pm		pm
Liverpool (Mount Pleasant)	dep.	7 *0		11 0	1 0	3 0			7 0
Manchester (Lower Mosley St.)	dep.	9 10	11 10	1 10	3 10	5 10	7 10		9 10
Oldham (Greaves St. G.P.O.)	,,	9 45	11 45	1 45	3 45	5 45	7 45		9 45
Uppermill (Commercial Hotel)	,,	10 0	12 0	2 0	4 0	6 0	8 0		10 0
Marsden (Tram Terminus)	,,	10 20	12 20	2 20	4 20	6 20	8 20		10 20
Huddersfield (Kirkgate)	,,	10 40	12 40	2 40	4 40	6 40	8 40		10 40
Liversedge (Swan Hotel)	,,	11 0	1 0	3 0	5 0	7 0	9 0		11 0
Leeds (Wellington St. 'Bus Stn.)	arr.	11 25	1 25	3 25	5 25	7 25	9 25		11 25
	dep.	11 35	1 35	3 35	5 35	7 35	9 35		
Selby (Market Place)	,,	12 25	2 25	4 25		8 25	10 25		
Howden (Memorial)	,,		2 50				10 50		
Hull (Paragon Street)	arr.		3 43				11 43		
Market Weighton (Griffin)	dep.	1 10		5 10		9 10			
Driffield (Buck Hotel)	,,	1 55		5 55		9 55			
Bridlington (Spa.)	arr.	2 25		6 25		10 25			
Tadcaster (White Swan)	dep.				6 15				
York (Piccadilly Stand)	,,				6 45				
Malton (Market Place)	,,				7 45				
Ganton (Greyhound Inn)	,,				8 20				
Scarborough ('Bus Sta., Vine St.)	arr.				8 50				

		am	am	am	am	pm	pm	pm	pm
Scarborough ('Bus Sta., Vine St.)	dep.					1 0			
Ganton (Greyhound Inn)	,,					1 30			
Malton (Market Place)	,,					2 5			
York (Piccadilly Stand)	,,					3 10			
Tadcaster (White Swan)	,,					3 40			
Bridlington (Spa)	,,			11 30		3 30		6 30	
Driffield (Buck Hotel)	,,			12 0		4 0		7 0	
Market Weighton (Griffin)	,,			12 45		4 45		7 45	
Hull (Paragon Street)	,,		9 50				5 50		
Howden (Memorial)	,,		11 0				7 0		
Selby (Market Place)	,,		11 25	1 30		5 30	7 25	8 30	
Leeds (Wellington St. 'Bus Stn.)	arr.		12 20	2 20	4 20	6 20	8 20	9 20	
	dep.	10 35	12 35	2 35	4 35	6 35	8 35		
Liversedge (Swan Hotel)	,,	7 20	11 0	1 0	3 0	5 0	7 0	9 0	
Huddersfield (Kirkgate)	,,	7 40	11 20	1 20	3 20	5 20	7 20	9 20	
Marsden (Tram Terminus)	,,	8 5	11 45	1 45	3 45	5 45	7 45	9 45	
Uppermill (Commercial Hotel)	,,	8 25	12 5	2 5	4 5	6 5	8 5	10 5	
Oldham (Greaves St. G.P.O.)	,,	8 45	12 25	2 25	4 25	6 25	8 25	10 25	
Manchester (Lower Mosley St.)	arr.	9 8	12 50	2 50	4 50	6 50	8 50	10 50	
Liverpool (Mount Pleasant)	arr.		2 55	4 55	6 55		10 55		

(Column note, right of times): Connects with 9·35 a.m. ex Leeds

* Not on Sundays.

For additional journeys between Manchester and Leeds, see pages 11 & 12.

These two pages from a North Western timetable of August 1929 show the remarkable hourly cross-Pennine service operated by the Limited Stop Pool in its first summer. The service numbers 61 and 61a were a paper exercise. The East Coast service brought in East Yorkshire instead of Northern, but had a chequered career before settling down as the all-year Liverpool - Middlesbrough service illustrated on page 47.

The winter timetable dated February 1930 included extra early and late journeys between Newcastle and Darlington, connected at this date by the Leeds & Newcastle company but not by United. However it seems likely that United would have accommodated one bus for the Pool overnight at its Darlington garage, at that time situated at Neasham Road.

The original "Tyne & Mersey" service was operated by Billy Ankers of Blaydon-on-Tyne who is probably standing in front of the bus in this picture at Marlborough Cresent, Newcastle. The date was 1928 when the Thornycroft bus **TY4418** was new, and the bus station on this site was yet to be built. *(West Newcastle Local Studies Collection, courtesy A.D.Walton)*

The typical coach of the Leeds & Newcastle Omnibus Company was the normal-control Gilford. This unidentified example was photographed in the Marlborough Crescent bus station in Newcastle, opened in 1929. The roof route board was particularly confusing. The large letters indicated a service between Ripon, Darlington and Newcastle without reference to Harrogate and Leeds, whilst the small letters showed places en route (Thirsk, Northallerton) as well as places served by connections (all the others). *(Fred Kennington Collection)*

2. References and Acknowledgements

The greater part of the information in this survey has been gained by the study of primary sources, i.e. official minutes, reports and timetables. Nevertheless it has also been necessary to use secondary sources for some details, and the authors acknowledge in particular their indebtedness to the printed works of Bruce Maund (both alone and with John Horne) and of Jim Soper. Extensive company records have been made available by the kind cooperation of the Manchester Museum of Transport and the West Yorkshire Information Service. Individual assistance has been generously given by Brian Biddiscombe, Peter Cardno, John Gill, Bob Kell, Alan Silcock, S.A.Staddon and especially John D.Watson who drew the map on page 5.

The following books have been helpful:-

Motor Coach Services from Merseyside 1920 to 1940, Part 1 The Independents, and Part 2 The Major Companies, by T.B.Maund
Liverpool Transport, Volumes 2, 4 and 5, J.B.Horne and T.B.Maund
Leeds Transport, Volume 2, Jim Soper
North Western, Volumes 1 and 2, Eric Ogden and Keith Healey
The Manchester Bus, Michael Eyre and Chris Heaps
Lancashire United, Eric Ogden
West Yorkshire, Keith A.Jenkinson
Northern Rose, Keith A.Jenkinson
Northern and its Subsidiaries, Keith A.Jenkinson and S.A.Staddon
The Omnibus, 'Coach Services on the Great North Road', J.Graeme Bruce.
ABC/BBF No. 9 Yorkshire Company Operators, B.C.Kennedy and P.J.Marshall

3. Stepping Stones

In the days before motorways, the choices for long distance travel were simple. Trains were quick but expensive. Buses were cheap, but even the express services were slow by comparision. The car was an option for only a few, and hardly came into consideration.

Vehicle development in the nineteen-twenties was rapid, and before the end of the decade comfortable coaches with pneumatic tyres and low frames were providing reliable long distance services. At their best, these coaches stopped only in major town centres, and the description "Express" was apt indeed. Only five years before, many lengthy journeys could only be accomplished by road in short sections provided by single-track-and-loop tramways or solid-tyred buses, and in more remote areas some stretches would have to be walked.

In 1923 you could travel the 35 miles between Liverpool and Manchester with three changes, departing from Liverpool by tram to Prescot and changing to a Crosville bus to Warrington. Here you would board a Lancashire United bus to Peel Green to connect with a

The Limited Stop services had begun to operate into the unfinished Worswick Street bus station in Newcastle on 15th May 1929. This official view, which may well have been taken to mark the station's completion in the July, shows North Western's **392 (DB5292)** ready to depart for Manchester. The bus was a Leyland-bodied TS1 and was in the fleet only from 1929 to 1931.

Salford Corporation tram to Deansgate in Manchester. The whole would take 3¼ hours. By 1927 LUT were operating through to Warrington from Manchester, and on 17th October 1928 Crosville commenced to operate from Warrington through to Liverpool (Mount Pleasant). Until then a change at Prescot was still required. An alternative route east from Warrington was by North Western bus to Altrincham, and Manchester Corporation tram into the city.

It might have been thought that a through service between Liverpool and Manchester would have been well established before anyone tackled the much more daunting proposition of a service all the way to Newcastle. Nevertheless the first coach services between Newcastle and Liverpool preceded the development of regular local services between the two great Lancashire cities. Whether they carried traffic between Liverpool and Manchester remains to be discovered, but it looks unlikely given the days and times of operation. The more obvious through service development seems to have been that of Ribble Motor Services from Seaforth via Liverpool to Manchester, commencing on 20th August 1928. The Manchester terminus was at the newly opened Lower Mosley Street bus station. How long the service operated is unclear, but it had finished by the end of 1928. On Sunday 28th October 1928 E.J.Jones's Imperial Motor Services of 308 Upper Parliament Street, Liverpool, was

due to commence a Liverpool - Manchester service with four departures a day from Brownlow Hill via Warrington and Irlam. There seems to be doubt that it operated; if so, it was only for a few days. Lancashire United were operating daily excursions from the Exchange Hotel, Manchester, to Liverpool during this period.

Crossing the Pennines from Lancashire to Yorkshire was one of the great feats of travel by road. One suggestion in 1923 for travel from Manchester to Leeds involved making ten tram and two bus connecting journeys via Todmorden, Halifax and Bradford, taking five hours altogether to cover about 55 miles. The alternative was the shorter route (about 46 miles) via Huddersfield and Bradford, which involved a seven-mile mountainous walk from Waterhead to Marsden but could otherwise be done entirely by tram.

There is a record of two Blackpool operators running a winter service during 1924-25 and 1925-26 from that resort to Manchester and Huddersfield, and perhaps local fares were available. By this time North Western had opened a depot in Oldham and commenced a service to Linthwaite (The Fountain Inn), which was the Huddersfield borough boundary. The service was advertised to commence on 8th April 1925, and had certainly done so by June. Although the tram service from Huddersfield ran through Linthwaite to Marsden, Huddersfield had no bus licensing powers

This "Overland" coach of Herbert Thomas Easton, Redcar, was a 1929 Leyland Lioness registered **DC9225**. The names displayed on the roof show the original Liverpool - Redcar route via York. It is notable that although the coach had two hinged doors, curtains and a roof luggage rack, it lacked the high-backed seats which would very shortly become the specific feature to distinguish a coach from a bus. The picture, much damaged, came from the Middlesbrough coachbuilding firm of W.G.Edmond, now Edmond & Milburn Ltd. *(With permission)*

An early scene at Lower Mosley Street, Manchester, included another of the short-lived North Western Leyland Tigers of 1929. The destination display on **409** (**DB9309**) was "Sankey, Prescot, Liverpool Limited Stop". Alongside, Tilling-Stevens **419** (**DB9319**) was preparing to depart for Hayfield. *(Authors' Collection)*

The Tilling-Stevens was also the choice for the Leeds & Newcastle company's new deliveries in 1930. Their VN2565 was lettered "Newcastle, Northallerton, Ripon, Harrogate, Leeds" and was the second of a pair with bodies by Chas. Roberts of Horbury. They subsequently joined the United fleet as P30 and P31. *(Senior Transport Archive)*

beyond Linthwaite, but refused to license North Western within Huddersfield. In the same period J.Hanson & Son started operating between Slaithwaite (The Star) and Huddersfield as from 29th May 1925. North Western continued to make applications for licences in Huddersfield. They had talks with Holdsworth Bros of Halifax (Hebble Bus Services) to try and overcome the problem, but without success. Consideration was given to purchasing land in Huddersfield and operating on a return ticket basis only. An appeal to the Minister of Transport was also considered. Licences were again refused in February 1928. The company was then informed by their parliamentary agent of the proposed bill by Huddersfield Corporation for powers to operate bus services outside the borough boundary, and an objection was lodged. This resulted in an agreement between North Western and the Corporation, whereby licences were granted on the condition that the company and its joint operators should not compete for local traffic within the Corporation area.

Beyond Huddersfield, the Corporation trams ran on the Leeds Road as far as Bradley. Three miles further on was Liversedge, and the Yorkshire (W.D.) Electric Tramways commenced a bus service in September 1923 from here to the Farnley trackless (i.e. trolleybus) terminus of the Leeds City Tramways. Twelve months later, the company was granted a three-month licence to run a bus service from Bradley tram terminus to Leeds, and a similar licence was granted to a firm called Scotia Motor Service. It is not known if these were taken up, but Yorkshire WD did commence a through service from Huddersfield to Leeds via Batley on 27th February 1925. On the alternative route to Leeds via Dewsbury, those two places were connected by a Yorkshire WD bus service from 22nd September 1924, and Robert Barr (of Wallace Arnold fame) commenced to run from nearby Birstall into Leeds on 21st October. It has also been said that Barr commenced a Leeds - Liverpool service on 3rd October 1926, but it is doubtful whether he ever ran such a service at all, let alone at a date so early for so lengthy a service.

When the intrepid early road traveller had reached Leeds, he was not yet halfway to Newcastle, and accomplishing the remaining 90 miles was in some ways more difficult than crossing the Pennines. A Leeds - Harrogate service was started on 4th June 1923 by A.Warburton of Leeds. The Harrogate Road Car Company commenced a similar service on 22nd December 1924. Beyond Harrogate to Ripon, a service had been started by United in June 1922, becoming joint with Harrogate & District in April 1925. A Ripon - Darlington licence granted to United does not seem to have been taken up. The 32-mile journey up the Great North Road through rich but sparsely populated agricultural land had to wait for the long distance services to be introduced. On the alternative route from Ripon to Darlington via Thirsk and Northallerton, United ran from Northallerton to Darlington, probably from 1923 or 1924, but the southerly section seems at this early stage to have had little more than rural market services. By the time United commenced to operate a Ripon to Northallerton local service on 19th September 1927, longer distance services which were eventually to become part of the Limited Stop Pool had already started, and United withdrew from this route at the end of June 1928. Northwards from Darlington, United ran to Durham from 1922, but via Bishop Auckland. On the direct road T.P.McDowell commenced a service from Darlington to Ferryhill in 1924 and James Walters, whom we shall meet later, did likewise in 1925. They jointly extended northwards to Durham on 30th August 1926. The final section northward from Durham was the earliest of any interurban section of the eventual Limited Stop services to be worked by motor buses. The Gateshead & District Tramways had commenced from Low Fell tram terminus to Chester-le-Street on 7th May 1913 and thence to Durham on 13th July. These workings were transferred to the new Northern company on 1st January 1914. The tram ride from Low Fell through Gateshead and into Newcastle, made possible by the linking of the Gateshead and Newcastle systems over the High Level Bridge on 12th January 1923, would complete the journey in the same way that it would have started from Liverpool.

It would be a hardy traveller indeed who would have chosen to make a long journey by bus in these circumstances. It took until 1927 even to have the links, so to speak, lying in a heap on the ground. It was then but a short step to make them up into 'chains' in the form of long distance services.

This page: These two splendid official Leyland pictures taken before the vehicle was registered show Overland's **XG253** of 1930. The Leyland-bodied Tiger was lettered "Liverpool, Manchester, Leeds, Stockton, Middlesbrough" and had a roof luggage rack, but the central rear emergency door, low-backed seats and lack of curtains added up to a specification which would soon be deemed inadequate for long distance work. *(Senior Transport Archive)*

>>> **Opposite page:** The through service between Hull and Liverpool had ceased by the end of 1934, but not before West Yorkshire's **544 (YG56)**, suitably inscribed, had been photographed at Lower Mosley Street in June 1934. The extensive roof board showed "Liverpool, Warrington, Manchester, Huddersfield, Leeds, Selby & Hull". The coach itself was a Leyland TS4 of 1932 with splendid Eastern Counties 28-seat bodywork. A through service between Hull and Liverpool was eventually reinstated by National Express in 1981. *(G H F Atkins)*

Another significant photograph, taken in 1935, was this one of Lancashire United's **246** (**TJ5744**), a new Dennis Arrow with Roe body. The rare feature is the "Overland Services" board displayed below the canopy, indicating that the bus was working the service acquired from Tyne & Mersey in October 1933 but not yet fully absorbed into the main Pool services. The destination blind simply stated "Liverpool via Bradford". *(Eric Ogden Collection)*

The flavour of prewar coaching on the Tyne - Tees - Mersey services is splendidly captured by this view of North Western's **601** (**JA2201**), one of 25 Eastern Counties-bodied Leyland TS4s of 1932. After 1934 they were accompanied on the Limited Stop services by similar United vehicles from their batch of 25 also supplied in 1932. *(Senior Transport Archive)*

4. The Independent Pioneers

As early as February 1927 a Gateshead solicitor was handling licence applications for a new company to be known as the **Leeds & Newcastle Omnibus Company Limited**, which proposed to operate between those two cities. The registered office was initially at 69 West Street, Gateshead, the premises of C.H.Mason & Co who were the main Gilford dealers in the north east. The service started on 3rd August 1927 and was managed by James Walters, whom we have already met. He was one of several directors of the LNOC who had other bus involvements in Co.Durham, an area renowned for its variety of partnerships and co-operatives. Significant features of the service were that it ran via Neville's Cross on the main road without going into Durham city, and that south of Darlington it ran via Northallerton and Thirsk. It was a stage service, albeit with some picking up restrictions, between Newcastle and Ripon, but served Harrogate and Leeds only on a return ticket basis. The Leeds terminus was on the premises of Wilks' Garage, Vicar Lane, and not on the public road.

Shortly after the start of the service, the LNOC applied to Middlesbrough for a service from that town to Leeds. The licence, not actually granted until 9th December 1927, was for operation every three hours via Stokesley. The service commenced on 12th January 1928. The rural character of the route via Stokesley soon led to operation by the slightly shorter and more populous route via Stockton instead, which was licensed on 15th February 1928. After some delay, this alteration was advertised to commence on 29th March 1928. Authority was granted in the summer of 1928 to reintroduce some journeys via Stokesley, but this does not seem to have been put into effect prior to May 1929, when Middlesbrough approved a 90-minute frequency alternately via Stokesley or Stockton. Indeed, it is not clear whether the company ever actually reinstated operation via Stokesley, despite being licensed to do so. The Middlesbrough to Leeds service operated as a feeder to the Newcastle service, which it met at Northallerton. This, the county town of the North Riding of Yorkshire, some sixteen miles south of Darlington, subsequently became the company's registered office and base of operations. This would ease the running of the Middlesbrough service, which at its nearest point was 34 miles away from the original base at Gateshead, although buses could no doubt be garaged with Walters and Johnson at Ferryhill, some 18 miles from Middlesbrough. In February 1930 it was noted that the company was by then operating from three depots, at Leeds, Northallerton and Durham.

A pioneer operator in Newcastle was the **Fawdon Bus Company Ltd**, registered on 23rd September 1927. Operations on a local service commenced that autumn with two Albion PM28 32-seaters TY3761/2, followed by a normal-control 26-seater registered TY3896. A Newcastle, Leeds, Birmingham and Coventry service was started, probably in July 1928 when two 26-seater Gilfords (CN3655/6) were added to the fleet. The route was via Boroughbridge rather than Ripon and Harrogate, and the picking up point in Leeds was Wilks' Garage. The daily journey did provide suitable timings for a day trip from Newcastle to Leeds, but not the other way round. This service subsequently played an important part in the history of the Limited Stop Pool. Four more vehicles augmented the fleet in 1928-29, a Leyland PLSC1 Lion WO1440, two more Albions and a Daimler. TY6375 was another normal control bus, and UA2326 a PM28. Gilford CN3655 was burned out in April 1929 and replaced by Daimler CF6 EF4091.

Another early operator was **Redwing Safety Services** of Redcar, who commenced a service from Thirsk to Harrogate via Ripon, Boroughbridge and Knaresborough on 30th March 1928. This partly replaced the short-lived Northallerton, Thirsk and Ripon service of R.W.Lancaster, who made things potentially confusing to historians by using the fleetname "Redline". The Redwing service from Middlesbrough commenced on 14th July 1928, with connections at Acklam (just south of Middlesbrough) from and to Stockton on the firm's existing service 1. Beyond Acklam, the route was via Stokesley, Northallerton, Thirsk and Ripon, and then via the direct road (Ripley and Killinghall) to Harrogate. The service was extended from Harrogate to Leeds on 18th September 1928. Like the LNOC, Redwing was not licensed to operate south of Ripon, and could carry only booked passengers on the Ripon - Leeds section. The Thirsk, Ripon, Knaresborough and Harrogate service (No.5) was withdrawn on 18th July 1929 and replaced by additional journeys between Middlesbrough and Leeds (No.7).

We can now be introduced to through operation between Newcastle and Liverpool. In

This dramatic 1934 action shot of the Limited Stop at work was taken in the centre of Harewood village with the entrance to Harewood House on the left. Another of North Western's TS4s of 1932, **595** (**DB9495**), was working south from Newcastle. West Yorkshire also operated a frequent Harrogate - Leeds local service along this stretch of road. *(Senior Transport Archive)*

Only the white wing tips and hooded headlamps give a visible clue that this picture was taken during the war. On Sunday 29th June 1941 the photographer was travelling to Newcastle from 'somewhere in the south' when at about 4.30pm the coach stopped at Catterick for the tea break. Northern's **865** (**CU3945**), a Brush-bodied Leyland TS8 of 1938, had Yorkshire Traction's **626** (**HE8916**) alongside, with Yorkshire Woollen District's service bus **444** (**HD6819**) bringing up the rear. A fourth coach was hiding in the back corner, and all were in convoy on the service from Coventry. *(J.C.Gillham)*

1927 trade papers reported that by November six limited stop services were operating between Tyneside and Manchester and Liverpool. Our guide to two of them is an unnamed author in 'Modern Transport' on 25th February 1928. On that date he presented the second of a series of articles written in a rather lurid style and describing his travels on that new phenomenon, the long distance motor coach. Earlier in the month he had travelled from Newcastle to Liverpool on a 20-seat Thornycroft operated by **William Ankers** of Blaydon. The driver, who was almost certainly Billy Ankers himself, explained that the first service from Newcastle to Liverpool had been commenced the previous autumn by Bunting and Taylor of Prudhoe, and ran thrice weekly. Mr Ankers decided to compete, and began a daily service in October 1927. Early in the new year Bunting and Taylor dropped out, and Ankers reduced his service for the remainder of the winter season to MWF from Newcastle and TuThS from Liverpool. Even so, on the chosen date our correspondent was the only passenger to make the full 170-mile through journey.

The Newcastle terminus was in Westmorland Road, adjacent to Marlborough Crescent where the bus station would be built in 1929. In Liverpool the terminus and booking office were at Hughes' Temperance Hotel at 18 Old Haymarket, until the buildings were demolished in 1929-30 to make way for the entrance to the Mersey Tunnel then under construction. The route was via Darlington, Ripon, Harrogate, Leeds, Huddersfield, Manchester and Warrington and the journey took 9 hours and 40 minutes, including breaks which totalled 65 minutes. The lunch stop was at the Chained Bull inn at Moortown, on the northern outskirts of Leeds.

At that time Ankers had three vehicles, an Associated Daimler 26-seater and two Thornycroft 20-seaters, one of which is recorded as PT9747 new in 1927. A new 29-seat Thornycroft registered TY4418 was added in May 1928, and this displayed posters headed "Tyne & Mersey" and showing the destinations "Newcastle on Tyne, Manchester, Liverpool". Thus it was Billy Ankers who coined the name *"Tyne & Mersey"* for this service, a name which was to last until the 1970s.

Herbert Thomas Easton lived on the sea front at 39 Newcomen Terrace, Redcar. His name first appeared in the Redcar Council Minutes in May 1908, when he was granted four hackney carriage licences. Even if these were horse-drawn conveyances, which seems likely, Easton had had up to twenty years experience of passenger transport by the time he applied for licences to run buses to Liverpool. On 11th May 1928 Middlesbrough council considered his application and noted that he did not yet have a bus for the proposed service, but they granted his application subject to his submitting satisfactory timetables. The service began in August, being advertised in the local press on 8th, although due to the summer recess the council did not record the licensing (to H.T.Easton & Sons) of the first bus, Albion 25-seater DC8541, until 14th September. Easton used the fleet name *"Overland"*. Further detail was recorded on 12th December 1928 when Stockton licensed him to operate via York, Leeds, Huddersfield and Manchester to Liverpool. Departure from Stockton was to be 9.30am on MWS and arrival back in the town at 4.30pm on TuThSu. The northbound journeys to Redcar left Liverpool at 8.15am, initially from Hughes' Temperance Hotel, Old Haymarket. An increase of frequency from thrice-weekly to daily was approved by Middlesbrough council in February and March 1929.

The year 1928 was a busy one for services between Liverpool and Newcastle as other, less successful, operators joined these pioneers. On 2nd May C.F.Rymer Ltd commenced a service from Liverpool to Durham, Sunderland, South Shields and Newcastle. The company had a garage at Chester-le-Street as well as in Liverpool. The service ceased for the winter in October 1928 and was never resumed. Also from May 1928, Eniway Motor Services of Manchester ran between Manchester and Newcastle. On 8th October Star Motors of Newcastle commenced a thrice-weekly "Nite" service. It was short lived. On 1st November 1928 Gladwyn Parlour Cars Ltd of Nottingham commenced a service from Liverpool to Newcastle, with two short workings to Leeds, but the service ceased with the business during December. The following winter, Said Hassan of South Shields started a South Shields, Newcastle and Liverpool service via Kirkby Stephen on 13th December 1929. Like many of the others, it did not last long. On the section between Newcastle and Leeds, another early operator was Heather Motor Service, not to be confused with the Robin Hood's Bay local operator of the same name. In this case the proprietor was W F Johnson, whose Billet Garage in Leeds was named after the Crooked Billet public house opposite Hunslet tram depot.

A

B

"HALL AUTOGRAPHIC MACHINE"

OUT **LIMITED STOP** IN
SERVICE

1 FROM *171C*
TO *LEEDS* 1

2 S. FARE D. CLASS
L6 2

DATE
6/8/84

3 L6 3

76567 4

SEE CONDITIONS ON BACK

LIMITED STOP
SERVICE.

From	Voucher No.
To	Class
S FARE D	
	Date

SEE CONDITIONS ON BACK

N1 36017

Bell Punch Company, Limited, London.

C

Northern General Transport Co., Ltd.

No.

Standage Voucher **1647**

.................................BUS STATION

DATE ....

VEHICLE REG. No..................../....................

SERVICE No...

TIME ENTERED or Station ....a.m.
Park p.m.

TIME LEAVING or Station ....a.m.
Park p.m.

DO YOU UNLOAD AT or Station ....
Park

DO YOU LOAD AT or Station ....
Park

Driver

PERSON ISSUING..

Conductor

D

Nº 4800 Ca

'LIMITED STOP SERVICE'

NEWCASTLE, MANCHESTER,
LIVERPOOL and HULL
Northern General Transport Co. Ltd.
West Yorkshire Road Car Co. Ltd.
The Yorkshire (W.D.) Electric Tramways
Co. Ltd.
North Western Road Car Co. Ltd.
East Yorkshire Motor Services Ltd.
Lancashire United Transport and Power
Co. Ltd.
United Automobile Services Ltd.

Date........................ Time............

Exchange Ticket
NO CASH VALUE

TICKET COLLECTED No. ....
AVAILABLE BETWEEN

....

AND

....

ON DAY OF ISSUE ONLY
CONDUCTOR'S INITIALS.............

Issued subject to the Companies' Regulations.
This Ticket has no cash value. To be produced
or given up on demand.
Williamson. Ticket Printer. Ashton-under-Lyne.

A selection of the tickets used on the Limited Stop over the years includes (**A**) the Hallgraphic, (**B**) the Bellgraphic or Automaticket, (**C**) conductor's standage voucher and (**D**) the book ticket, all of which required the conductor to write on the ticket in indelible pencil. The eventual use of the Speed Setright machine (**E**) eliminated the need for the pencil. The book ticket dates from the very short period in 1935 when both East Yorkshire and United were named.

E

20

His service to Newcastle ran from November 1927 to July 1929. There was also Smith's Safeway Services (Middlesbrough) covering the Darlington to Harrogate section with its seasonal Middlesbrough - Blackpool service from 1928, and Diamond Road Coaches of South Moor, Stanley, Co.Durham, who operated a Sheffield - Newcastle service via Leeds from October 1928. Other operators including J.M.Calvert (Crook), Central Motor Coach Services (Manchester), A.E.Elliott (Newcastle), Finglands (Manchester), Hall Bros (Morpeth), MacShanes (Liverpool), Manchester General, Merseyside Touring Company, Edward Page (Blyth), G.W.Rennie (Sunderland), Ribble and United (joint service via Skipton), Underwood of Sunderland, and Wansbeck Trading Association (Ashington) applied for licences between Liverpool and the North East in 1928-30. Similarly, the Mid Yorkshire and South Durham Omnibus Services (base not known) and Smith's Safeway Services (Middlesbrough) applied to operate between Middlesbrough and Leeds. Some were granted, but none of them operated.

The significant pioneer who was not independent was the **Northern** company. Their contribution began on 1st May 1928 with what they described as a "Daily Pleasure Trip to Liverpool from Newcastle and to Newcastle from Liverpool." Single and return fares were offered, and Leeds, Manchester and perhaps other intermediate points were also served. The trips were operated with S.O.S. charabancs, and over such a long distance the term "endurance test" might have seemed more appropriate than "pleasure trip". Despite the image of a day excursion, there could have been no question of going there and back in the same day. In Liverpool, Northern (as well as Rymer's) terminated at Brownlow Hill at the side of the Adelphi Hotel. In Leeds, the service operated from the Corn Exchange premises of Wallace Arnold, who also acted as Northern's agents. It is probable, particularly in the light of a report in Motor Transport on 29th October 1928, that the services said to have been operated by Wallace Arnold from Leeds to Liverpool and to Newcastle were actually Northern's. It soon became apparent to Northern that a timetabled bus service was required, and the development of the Limited Stop Pool was built on the foundation of this experience.

5. *Establishing the Pool Services*

a) *Liverpool to Manchester*

In late 1928 Crosville, Lancashire United and North Western had discussed proposals for a joint service between the two cities. However, local licensing was not easy. Manchester and Liverpool granted licences to all three operators for an hourly service alternately via Eccles and Altrincham. Eccles, in the Lancashire United agreed area, would not grant licences to North Western or Crosville, and Altrincham in North Western's territory would not license Lancashire United or Crosville. By 28th March 1929, when the service was due to commence, the matter had still not been resolved. In the end North Western operated via Altrincham only, and Lancashire United via Eccles only. Crosville's part would have consisted of four return trips. The licensing refusals resulted in gaps in the timetable where those journeys would have operated. Thus, however unsatisfactorily, the first part of the Limited Stop chain was completed.

b) *Manchester to Leeds*

During late 1928 meetings had been held with various associated companies regarding limited stop services from Manchester to the south and north-east. For the services to the north-east two routes were proposed. 'Route 4' was to be Manchester, Rochdale, Halifax, Leeds, Harrogate, Ripon, Stockton, Middlesbrough, West Hartlepool, Sunderland and Newcastle. 'Route 5' was to be Manchester, Oldham, Huddersfield, Leeds, Harrogate, Ripon, Darlington, Durham and Newcastle. By February 1929 the decision had been reached to operate 'route 5' only.

By December 1928 the licence applications by the associated companies were already going ahead. Huddersfield had granted a licence on 19th January 1929 for a joint service between Manchester and Newcastle, to be operated by North Western, Northern, West Yorkshire and Yorkshire WD. While waiting for other towns to grant licences, North Western commenced its own service between Manchester and Huddersfield, commencing on 28th March 1929. This connected at Manchester with the Liverpool service which, as we have already seen, commenced on the same day. The Oldham - Linthwaite service was withdrawn at the same time. At last on 15th May 1929 the service was

For several years after the resumption of the Limited Stop services in 1946, prewar vehicles continued to be the mainstay of their operation. The point is well illustrated by two pictures of outwardly similar United buses at Harrogate on a busy summer's day in 1952. In the view above, **BJ21** (**BHN217**), a 1936 Bristol JO5G, was working to Leeds, but it and the similar vehicle behind were almost empty. Heavy duplication was probably required on the return journey to Middlesbrough. Working in that direction *(>>> opposite page)* was the 1931 AEC Regal **AR5** (**VY2551**), handsomely rebodied by Eastern Coach Works in 1937 and still sporting a full set of glass draught deflectors over the windows. As the signals suggest, the railway station was immediately adjacent, and Harrogate had the ideal bus and train connecting facility.*(Both: R F Mack Collection)*

extended via Liversedge to Leeds and thence to Newcastle after pressure had been put on various licensing authorities.

c) Leeds to Newcastle

Further north, Newcastle gave the first decision when it refused on 4th January. Darlington agreed on 24th January to grant licences (to Northern) but did not give a commencement date. Ripon granted a licence on 30th January, Leeds refused on 6th February, and Harrogate was still deciding. Pressure was put on Leeds and Newcastle to reconsider, and by May the four operators North Western, Northern, West Yorkshire and Yorkshire WD were all licensed. The joint service commenced between Manchester and Newcastle on 15th May, which in conjunction with the Manchester - Liverpool service completed the chain coast to coast. A particular strength which the Pool companies enjoyed from the beginning was the use of Lower Mosley Street bus station in Manchester. It was owned by Omnibus Stations Ltd in which North Western and Ribble each held a 35.7% share, with eight other operators together variously holding the remaining 28.6%. It provided accommodation and connecting facilities which the small firms could not match.

6. Manchester to Newcastle and the East Coast, 1929

The original mileage worked between Manchester and Newcastle was divided equally among the four operators, with each running two vehicles daily. The route out of Oldham was via Lees and Uppermill before rejoining the main road at the appropriately named Bleak Hey Nook and tackling the climb to 1270 feet at Standedge. After Huddersfield the route initally continued on the main road through Liversedge to Leeds. There were also to be short workings between Manchester and Leeds with two vehicles provided by North Western and one by West Yorkshire. There is as yet no clear evidence that these additional journeys commenced before 6th July 1929. However, on that date the proposed short workings were incorporated into extensions from Leeds to Scarborough, to Bridlington and to Hull. The Scarborough service was operated by North Western and West Yorkshire with one journey daily in each direction. The Hull service brought in East Yorkshire as a joint operator, with two journeys daily in each direction via Selby and Howden. The Bridlington service also included East Yorkshire, but all passengers had to change at Leeds. Return tickets were inter-available

between Manchester and Leeds among all the five operators. The commencement of these services on 6th July coincided with the opening of West Yorkshire's coach station in Wellington Street, Leeds. The company had purchased the site in the January. It enabled them to comply with Leeds City Council's insistence that long distance services must not pick up and set down in the streets of the city. It also put them in a strong position in relation to other operators in the same way that Lower Mosley Street did in Manchester.

On 11th May 1929 the Merseyside Touring Company had commenced a Liverpool - Scarborough service via Manchester and Leeds with intermediate fares. It was discontinued at the end of October. In order to meet the competition from other operators, the Pool offered connecting facilities at Manchester from Liverpool on all the services to Leeds and beyond, with through fares. The services to Bridlington, Scarborough and Hull were suspended at the end of the 1929 summer period, and East Yorkshire withdrew from the mileage pool. Short workings were still operated between Manchester and Leeds, and a revised service to Newcastle was run from 6th October.

7. 1930 - Extension and Competition

For the 1930 season the services to Bridlington and Scarborough were replaced by a single service to Scarborough via Bridlington operated by North Western only. The last picking up point from Manchester was Marsden, and it was then non-stop to the coast. The service to Hull was not reinstated in 1930, and passengers had to change to or from East Yorkshire's separate Leeds - Hull service. It was also decided to extend two daily journeys from Newcastle right through to Liverpool, and vice versa. These were operated by North Western via Altrincham, to avoid upsetting the mileage arrangements. Although Crosville had still not participated on the Liverpool and Manchester service, North Western and Lancashire United now operated an hourly service via Eccles or Altrincham.

By this time other operators were adding to the existing competitors on various parts of the route. J.Hanson was granted licences for a two-hourly service between Huddersfield and Oldham. Merseyside recommended their Liverpool - Scarborough service on 1st April 1930, and introduced a daily service to Great Yarmouth on 14th April with fares between Liverpool and Manchester. Later in the year International Express introduced a thrice daily service from Liverpool to Nottingham via Manchester, also with local fares. Tyne & Mersey and Overland were still operating from Newcastle and Redcar respectively to Liverpool, and Leeds & Newcastle Omnibus Co from both Middlesbrough and Newcastle to Leeds. The Fawdon Bus Co continued to operate between Newcastle, Leeds and Coventry, Redwing Safety Services between

The takeover of the Fawdon company in 1933 brought the Pool operators on to the Leeds - Coventry road. In a busy scene at Derby bus station, two Northern buses were working south. They were Leyland TS7/Roe **1313** and **1315** (**HD5821/3**) of 1936, purchased from Yorkshire WD in 1949. In the opposite direction, Yorkshire Traction's HE8900 was bound for Hull, and the picture is completed by a distinctive East Yorkshire Leyland PS1 bodied by Eastern Coach Works. *(R N Hannay)*

Redcar and Leeds, and Smith's Safeway seasonally between Middlesbrough and Blackpool. In June 1930 Ribble Motor Services of Preston purchased the Merseyside company. They operated it as a subsidiary until February 1932, when all the licences were transferred to Ribble.

The Newcastle service flourished despite the competition, as was demonstrated in the Manchester holidays on Saturday 26th July 1930. That day saw twenty North Western duplicates being operated, of which eight stayed overnight in Newcastle, returning on the Sunday. It is of note that North Western did not operate any duplicates to Newcastle on the Sunday, these being supplied by other pool operators who had stayed over in Manchester on Saturday night.

8. The 1930 Road Traffic Act, Lancashire United and East Yorkshire

Nothing of note happened to the services in the 1930-31 winter period, but there was a lot of activity behind the scenes. The passing of the Road Traffic Act 1930 meant that important changes were on the way. Most significant was the change in the granting of licences. This was to be the province of the new Traffic Commissioners instead of the local authorities. The Act came into force on 1st April 1931. To obtain licences, operators had to have applied to the Traffic Commissioners prior to 31st March 1931. They also had to have been operating their services from at least 9th February 1931, if they were to be allowed to continue them while waiting for their applications to be considered. This did generally bring a surge of new services in late 1930 to beat the deadline, and from it we can deduce that the inclusion of a variation of some journeys via Dewsbury was introduced in 1930. On the other hand, the through service to Hull had not operated in 1930 and so did not operate in 1931 either.

The applications lodged by the Pool were as follows:-

1) Manchester - Newcastle as operated in 1930, amended to extend the route to and from Liverpool and to include Lancashire United as a joint operator.
2) Manchester - Hull. This application was to join up East Yorkshire's Hull - Leeds service with the Pool's Leeds - Manchester service, later amended to extend to Liverpool and to include LUT

When this photograph was taken on 23rd July 1949, the use of double deck duplicates between Manchester and Liverpool was in anticipation of the Traffic Commissioners' permission. North Western's **947** (**AJA147**) with its original coach-seated ECW body was loading at Lower Mosley Street, Manchester, and carried a makeshift paper destination label. *(Keith Healey)*

as in no.1. East Yorkshire would be a joint operator on this route only.

3) Manchester - Liverpool application by North Western and Lancashire United only, to operate jointly as in 1930.

4) Manchester - Liverpool application by Crosville Motor Services, to operate as in 1930 but with no mention of joint operation.

The Manchester - Liverpool applications also included an additional hourly SSuBH service in between the normal daily services applied for. In the Northern TA, the backing licences were granted on 14th May 1931.

The revised services were to commence from 14th March 1932. The licences allowed for a new picking up point at Warrington, with a restriction on carrying passengers from that town to either Liverpool or Manchester. The North Western and LUT licence (3) was amended to operate SSuBH only, with the other timings being transferred to either the Newcastle or Hull licences. On the Huddersfield - Leeds section, the Newcastle journeys were revised to operate via Dewsbury, whilst the Hull journeys and the short workings to Leeds went via Liversedge, i.e. the converse of the previous arrangement. The Dewsbury and Altrincham variations were paired together, as were Liversedge and Eccles, which was also the converse of the previous situation.

The grant did show how different Traffic Commissioners worked. There had been through bookings available, involving changing to local services at Durham for the Sunderland area, Chester-le-Street for Stanley and Consett, Newcastle for South Shields, Dewsbury for Ossett and Batley, and Liversedge for Cleckheaton and Heckmondwike. The Northern TC granted the facilities in their area, but Yorkshire TC refused them and required passengers to pay separately on the connecting bus or tram.

In the same period three licences were granted to competitors on 1st August 1931. The Leeds & Newcastle Omnibus Co was licensed to operate Newcastle - Leeds and Middlesbrough - Leeds, and Redwing was also licensed for Middlesbrough - Leeds. For the now-combined Tyne & Mersey and Overland operation (*described below in section 11*), H.T.Easton applied for two routes, Newcastle - Liverpool and Redcar - Liverpool, the latter via Darlington. On 17th September 1931 the service from Newcastle was granted, but the other was permitted only as a Redcar - Darlington feeder to the Newcastle route. However International Express were not so lucky with their Liverpool - Nottingham service. They carried 26,000 passengers in 1931, but Yorkshire TA refused them a licence, though both North Western TA

Northern's 1938 Leyland TS8 869 (CU3949) had just had the radiator topped up after its journey from Liverpool when this picture was taken at Lower Mosley Street, Manchester, and the North Western conductor was getting a breath of fresh air or, more likely, a smoke. Perhaps he was wondering how the coach would fare on its climb over the Pennines? This was an early example of the vehicle running through but the crew changing over at Leeds. *(Keith Healey)*

and East Midland TA granted the service. The service ceased and the company went into liquidation on Monday 25th April 1932 after losing an appeal.

9. Mileage and Territories

On 9th January 1932 the Pool mileage was agreed among the operators as follows:-

Manchester - Newcastle equally between North Western, West Yorkshire, Yorkshire WD and Northern;
Manchester - Liverpool equally between Lancashire United, North Western and Crosville; and
Manchester - Hull equally between North Western, West Yorkshire, Yorkshire WD and East Yorkshire.

Receipts were to be divided pro rata to miles run.

By this time the territory of each operator had been agreed where relevant with other operators and with the railway companies. The Limited Stop to Newcastle operated through seven different areas:-

Liverpool - Warrington, Crosville (Independent, then railway owned, now TBAT);
Warrington - Manchester via Eccles, LUT (Independent);
Warrington - Manchester via Altrincham, North Western (BAT, now TBAT);
Manchester - Huddersfield, North Western (BAT, now TBAT);
Huddersfield - Leeds, Yorkshire WD (BET);
Leeds - Ripon, West Yorkshire (BAT, now TBAT);
Ripon - Durham, United (Independent, now TBAT); and
Durham - Newcastle, Northern (BET).

In several cases, the operators had gone through significant changes of ownership, as the list shows. The British Electric Traction companies had tramway origins, and indeed the Gateshead and Yorkshire WD systems were still running. On the other hand, the British Automobile Traction firms were members of a group established by the BET specifically for motor bus operation. They were subsequently party to a Tilling involvement which created the Tilling & British Automobile Traction group.

Another coach of the same type was 866 (CU3966) photographed in pristine condition at Harrogate, complete with roof route boards. These display "Newcastle, Leeds, Huddersfield, Manchester, Liverpool", not quite as comprehensive as prewar examples, but less cluttered and perhaps more effective. *(C F Klapper)*

By this time in the Pool's history, there was also significant railway involvement in these holding companies. The complexity of controlling groups and systems meant that the management of the Pool services was at times slow and cumbersome.

10. 1932 Developments

For the 1932 season Ribble's ex-Merseyside service to Scarborough was rerouted via St.Helens, Bolton and Halifax to avoid Manchester. At the same time the first setting down point from Liverpool on their Great Yarmouth service was Stockport instead of Manchester.

United and Eastern Counties commenced a joint Newcastle - Leeds - Lowestoft summer service in 1932, with one daily journey each way. It was designated 50 by United and S by Eastern Counties. The Newcastle terminus was Haymarket, and coaches did not call at Northern's Worswick Street bus station. In other respects it followed the Pool route via Ripon and Harrogate to Leeds, but apparently independently of the Pool services and without detriment to them. Ironically it was the much longer Leeds - Lowestoft section which came in later years to be linked to the Pool services, as mentioned below in section 27.

Problems arose in Liverpool with the agent who acted for Lancashire United. Avery & Roberts were originally coach operators but had had their fleet taken over by the War Department in 1914. They came to an agreement with LUT in 1919 whereby they would act as their representatives in Liverpool and use only LUT vehicles. As motor dealers they occupied half of the garage in Bentley Road, Princes Park, which LUT had purchased in August of that year. In 1932 they went into liquidation owing North Western £172 for bookings to Newcastle. The Pool decided to write off this amount. Lancashire United took over the booking office in Renshaw Street, which with the garage in Bentley Road became directly operated by LUT. The Pool vehicles were subsequently garaged at Bentley Road overnight.

On Saturday 3rd December 1932 North Western commenced a new stage carriage service between Oldham and Huddersfield. This permitted the removal of local fares between Oldham and Marsden on the Pool service. The new service was co-ordinated with the existing Hanson service to provide an hourly service (every two hours for each operator) but it was not a joint service.

11. 1928-33 - Development of Leeds & Newcastle, Redwing, Overland and Tyne & Mersey

The **Leeds & Newcastle** company remained fairly constant in its operations in this period, with just two developments of note. At the start of the 1929 summer season, Middlesbrough had in May approved a 90-minute frequency operating to Leeds alternately via Stokesley or Stockton, as we saw above in section 4. It probably never operated in that form, although the increase in frequency was implemented in

A further example of double deck operation shows North Western's **216** (**CDB216**) at Manchester. By the time this picture was taken, the appropriate destination displays were available on double deckers, and 216 shows "Liverpool, Warrington, Eccles". On its left, Lancashire United's **191** (**KTB104**) is bound for Middlesbrough, whilst on the right is North Western's rebodied **676** (**JA2276**) for Barnsley. The Pool offered through Liverpool - Barnsley bookings to this service, with daily through buses in summer, and this may well have been one of them. *(Keith Healey)*

Northern's **931** (**CN9231**) was a classy touring coach when new in 1939 but was hard at work on the Pool services when photographed in Feethams, Darlington, in 1951. In the absence of blinds, Northern's unusual circular paper destination labels showed that the coach was running to Barnsley and Coventry on this occasion. *(A B Cross)*

June, because in that month the company was licensed by both Stockton and West Hartlepool to extend northwards from Stockton to West Hartlepool and Sunderland. These extended journeys would have to omit Middlesbrough, which for a journey from Northallerton to Sunderland was awkwardly placed on the Yorkshire side of the River Tees. However, the extension to Sunderland was short lived, and finished on Saturday 12th April 1930. The workings were cut back to Stockton, and by 1st August the timetable showed a 90-minute frequency between Stockton and Leeds with alternate journeys extending to or from Middlesbrough. The Northallerton to Leeds section was, as before, on the same timings as the Newcastle to Leeds service. The licences granted by the Traffic Commissioners in August 1931 retained this arrangement at Northallerton, but reduced the frequency to two-hourly, with all the connecting journeys operating through to Middlesbrough via Stockton.

The other LNOC development was of through bookings to Blackpool. This was effected in June 1930 by a Leeds connection at Wilks' Garage arranged with Progress Motors (W.Armitage & Sons Ltd) of County Garage, Dickson Road, Blackpool. They were the only operator at this time to run all year between Blackpool and Leeds, and had two daily departures each way.

Although in April 1929 *Redwing* had been granted a reduction by Middlesbrough from seven to five daily departures to Leeds, on 12th July 1929 an increased frequency of eight journeys was approved. The overall result was an untenable combined frequency of sixteen journeys per day, with four LNOC runs via Stockton, and four LNOC and all eight Redwing via Stokesley. A year later, on 11th June 1930, Stockton council licensed Redwing to operate between Middlesbrough and Leeds via Stockton, but the extent of this operation was not stated, although there is evidence that it took place. In 1931, the service applied for and granted by the Traffic Commissioners was via Stokesley, with no journeys via Stockton, yet by the November, when the company became a wholly-owned subsidiary of United, six daily journeys were operated, two of them via Stockton. A few years later, when the Redwing and LNOC services had been completely absorbed into the Pool, as will be described below, all journeys operated via Stockton. When we consider that the journey via Stockton was a little bit shorter and was serving a large industrial town, it seems strange indeed that the Pool's antecedents should have involved such an intensive service running instead via the small market town of Stokesley. Perhaps the local licensing committees were more influential than we are nowadays led to believe?

William Ankers added another Thornycroft (UP1817) to his fleet in September 1928, and a Gilford (UP2289) in March 1929. The sale of TY4418 to Sunderland Corporation in November 1929 was probably a sign of economic difficulties, for on 24th March 1930 Ankers assigned the operation to a trustee. This was the prelude to the sale of his "Tyne & Mersey" Liverpool service to H.T.Easton. It seems likely that Easton took over the actual operation of the service in March 1930. On 4th April 1930, Middlesbrough council licensed Easton to revise his own route from Redcar. Between Stockton and Leeds he had hitherto run via Thirsk and York, but he now changed it to run via Darlington, Catterick, Ripon and Harrogate. This brought him to meet the Newcastle - Liverpool route at the nearest possible point, namely Darlington, and whenever feasible he could combine the two loads and use only the one bus between Darlington and Liverpool. Another alteration approved at the same time was to operate the Leeds - Huddersfield section via Bradford instead of direct. An application to Darlington for the revision to run his Redcar - Liverpool service via that town was heard as early as 20th March but refused on 17th April.

Billy Ankers retained at least one bus, with which he operated a local service between Blaydon and Newcastle. The bus was the Thornycroft PT9747, pioneer of his Liverpool service. Indeed he had even named his house "Thornycroft", but United took over his service on 29th August 1930 and bought the bus. After this, Ankers worked as a driver at the Addison, Blaydon, depot from which United was operating the former Emmerson's network.

Completion of the purchase by Easton of the Tyne & Mersey service was achieved on 30th June. He then proceeded to register *Tyne & Mersey Motor Services Limited*, as from 13th August 1930. The company's capital consisted of 1,500 £1 shares. It would be expected that the new company's name would now predominate, but apparently it did not. When the licensing provisions of the 1930 Road Traffic Act began to take effect, Easton made application as *"Herbert Thomas Easton, Overland Services"* for licences to continue his existing services.

These were published in Notices & Proceedings for the Northern TA on 16th April 1931 as TAR365/1 Newcastle - Darlington - Liverpool and TAR365/2 Redcar - Darlington - Liverpool. On 17th September the Commissioners granted TAR365/1 in full, but the other only as a Redcar - Darlington feeder service. When the Liverpool terminus at Hughes' Temperance Hotel, Old Haymarket, was withdrawn, the Tyne & Mersey and Overland services were transferred to the opposite end of William Brown Street at MacShanes, 5 Commutation Row, in the corner of Islington and London Road opposite Lime Street. This apparently occurred in 1931.

On the vehicle front, Easton added a Leyland 25-seater (DC9225) licensed in June 1929 and a Leyland Tiger 26-seater (XG253) twelve months later. A Crossley 28-seat coach supplied to "Overland of Redcar" was registered XG925 in May 1931. It is thought to have been the same vehicle as the Alpha with chassis number 90629 originally registered as VR8750 circa May 1930. In June 1931 Easton issued a separate timetable for his Redcar - Liverpool service as if the Newcastle service did not exist. Later in the same year, perhaps after the issue of the licences, he produced a combined timetable for both services. Both were headed "Overland", with no reference to Tyne & Mersey.

Easton did not pay dues for the use of the Exchange bus station in Middlesbrough after 1st April 1932. Four weeks later, on 28th, both licences were granted a variation consisting of a change of name from H.T.Easton to Tyne & Mersey Motor Services Ltd, and in June the Tyne & Mersey company applied to continue the Easton licences. What appears to have happened is that Easton sold the Tyne & Mersey company, and with it the "Overland" operation, probably in April 1932. The new proprietors included T.H.Allen of Blyth. They were hardly going to use Easton's own name after they had bought his Tyne & Mersey company, but it is significant that the change of name was not a change of licence. The services continued to be licensed as TAR365/1 and 365/2. After these

grants, Tyne & Mersey applied on 30th July 1932 for an excursion and tour licence originating at Liverpool (St.John's Lane) with one destination - Blackpool, for the period of the illuminations only. On 20th August they also applied for additional journeys on the Newcastle service, departing 10.30pm nightly in each direction. Both applications were refused. Rumours were also afoot that the business was for sale, and that Red & White of Chepstow were interested.

A 1932 timetable leaflet coupled the "Overland Services - operated by Tyne & Mersey Motor Services Ltd" with the Newcastle - Aberdeen service of T.Allen & Sons of Blyth. Both had the same Newcastle address of 6 Haymarket, and both had the same telephone number. Two new 30-seat Tyne & Mersey coaches acquired in the summer of 1932 were AEC Regals registered by Northumberland as TY9817/27, no doubt from Allen's address in Blyth rather than from the T&M office in Newcastle. They replaced the two ex-Easton Leylands. The Tyne & Mersey and Overland names were both displayed on the new coaches. In the autumn of that year, proposals were in hand for a merger between Tyne & Mersey, T. Allen & Sons and County Motor Services Ltd of Choppington, Northumberland. It came to nothing when County signed on 2nd January 1933 to sell their London, Newcastle, Edinburgh and Glasgow services to United and SMT.

One of your authors is grateful to the late Matthew Leslie who warmly described Billy Ankers as a kindly man and a good friend. The two were colleagues with United at Addison in 1930-32. Likewise, the late Arnold Hadfield spoke of Herbert Easton who, years later, was a next door neighbour in Borough Road, Redcar, and who described in lively terms those early years on the Liverpool service. Mr.Leslie and Mr Hadfield both died in 1999, but not before they had helped to make it seem as if those pioneering days of seventy years ago were as near as last week.

<<< *Opposite page:* Most of the vehicles shown in this remarkable view of the coach station at Leeds in April 1952 were prewar. Exceptions were three Northern Guys, which with their cramped 38 seats must have been the most uncomfortable buses on offer. Centre stage was held by West Yorkshire's **194** (**DWW599**) and the extreme wings were graced by North Western and Yorkshire WD Leylands. Lined up against the back wall were six Northern and two North Western vehicles. The latter's destinations are of particular interest. To the right, the rebodied **678** (**JA2278**) displayed "Middlesbrough", to which town the company's buses would only run at bank holiday peaks, and on the left an unidentified Bristol L5G thought it was going to Marple and Hayfield. *(G H F Atkins)*

Crosville's early attempts to be involved in the Limited Stop Pool on account of its territorial possession of the Liverpool - Warrington section achieved very little, but the Company was heavily involved with the linked Llandudno services in the postwar period. In this scene at Lower Mosley Street, Manchester, **KA193** (**FM7472**) was "On Hire to North Western" on such a journey. It had come from Llandudno and would run through to Leeds as a duplicate to the 12.43pm Pool departure. The coach itself was unusual, being a reconditioned 1933 Leyland TS4 rebodied in classic style by Eastern Coach Works. *(Keith Healey)*

Two rather more modern Crosville coaches labelled "On Hire to North Western" were on the Bristol LWL6B chassis, seated 35 and were new in 1951. Nearer the camera was **KW266** (**MFM697**) at Lower Mosley Street, Manchester. This was a late afternoon picture. The coaches had already run from North Wales to Leeds, and had returned on the 3.25pm departure. After a short break here, they would continue as duplicates to North Western's 5.45pm journey to Llandudno. *(Keith Healey)*

12. 1930-33 - The Involvement of United

The United company had been approached at the beginning in 1928/29, but had declined to join the Pool, and had simply accepted fare protection over its local routes. After a hotly contested change in the company's ownership in 1929, United took part in a Pool meeting on 8th November 1930. United suggested that it was now time for them to join the Pool. Their argument was that a great deal of the mileage was operated in their territory. The Pool members stated that although the length of road was considerable, the territory was very sparsely populated and perhaps United should consider bringing something of greater value into the Pool. Two suggestions were made, a service between Leeds and Newcastle via Darlington, Stockton, Middlesbrough, West Hartlepool and Sunderland, or an extension of the Pool service northwards to Glasgow and Edinburgh. United said they would consider these points. It was not until May 1933 that they put forward their ideas.

At a meeting held at Leeds on 2nd May 1933 it was resolved by the Pool members:-

1) To include the joint United and West Yorkshire Leeds - Middlesbrough service in the Pool.
2) To include the services of the Leeds & Newcastle Omnibus Co with whom United had recently signed a purchase agreement.
3) To purchase the Tyne & Mersey service.
4) To apply for a two-hourly service Liverpool - Newcastle.
5) To apply for a two-hourly service Liverpool - Middlesbrough.

United then proposed the following:-

1) United and West Yorkshire to participate to the extent of their full annual mileage between Leeds, Middlesbrough and Redcar.
2) United to discontinue the LNOC service between Leeds and Middlesbrough but to retain certain LNOC local services which were entirely in the United area.
3) United to discontinue the LNOC service between Leeds and Newcastle, provided they were allowed to participate as in no.1.

4) The Pool to pay United £5,000 for the LNOC business including eight Gilford coaches.

It was agreed to accept United's proposals and to draw up a new timetable to be submitted to the Traffic Commissioners. United were also to be offered a share in the Tyne & Mersey service to enable them to participate in the mileage run.

At this point a review of United's activities will explain how in three years the situation had changed so much. The company was fiercely independent under its founder E.B.Hutchinson and was a formidable enterprise. In July 1929 the LNER and TBAT acquired equal controlling shareholdings in United. Here and elsewhere the LNER then decided to transfer its various local bus interests to the big territorial operator. In the case of Redwing Safety Services of Redcar, the operation became a wholly-owned subsidiary of United in November 1931. On its Middlesbrough - Leeds stage service there were several sections where local passengers were not carried, notably between Ripon and Leeds. Northbound passengers boarding the Redwing service in Leeds or Harrogate had to be in possession of return tickets. The service was numbered 7, but in June or July 1932 it became number 60 in United's comprehensive route renumbering scheme. At this stage four of the six daily return journeys still operated via Stokesley, and the other two via Stockton. The service was transferred to United on 31st August 1932, when it became a joint express service with West Yorkshire, retaining the number 60, and with all journeys running via Stockton. It operated through from Redcar in the following summer seasons. The involvement of West Yorkshire brought an end to the Ripon - Leeds restrictions which had affected the Redwing company, and also saw the transfer of the Leeds terminus from Vicar Lane to Wellington Street. The service could now be advertised as providing connections for Manchester and Liverpool. Redwing had operated the Northallerton - Thirsk section via the villages of Otterington and Sand Hutton, and the Thirsk - Ripon section similarly via Rainton. United used the main A168 between Northallerton and Thirsk, and thence to Ripon operated via Dishforth. To cover the omitted villages, a new but sparse United local service 19 between Northallerton, Thirsk and Ripon was also introduced on 31st August 1932.

During the war many coaches were rebuilt as service buses, and in the early postwar years there was a severe shortage of coaches. Northern's Guy Arab **1090** (**GUP90**) was a modern vehicle when photographed on the Limited Stop at Darlington in 1948, but with its 38 cramped seats was seriously unsuitable for the nine-hour journey from Newcastle to Liverpool. *(C F Klapper)*

The brave new world of postwar Britain offered wonderful clarity when it came to Tilling Group bus destination displays. The prospect of an eight-hour journey on a Bristol L5G service bus was not quite so dashing, but it was often the best that was available, as when United's **BLO193** (**GHN993**) was photographed behind the bus station at Park Street, Middlesbrough. *(United)*

13. 1933 - Newcastle to Coventry, the Fawdon Bus Company

Meanwhile there was an important take-over that affected the Pool and which comes into the story at this point. The Fawdon Bus Co Ltd operated a service between Newcastle and Coventry, as mentioned above in section 4. In the usual manner they applied in April 1931 to continue the service, and the Northern TA granted a licence on 1st October 1931. The company's address in this period was Percy Chambers, 33 Percy Street, Newcastle.

The Yorkshire Services Pool operated from various parts of Yorkshire to Birmingham and London, and by 1933 the constituent companies were West Yorkshire, Yorkshire WD, Yorkshire Traction and East Yorkshire. As a member of both the Limited Stop and Yorkshire Services Pools, the West Yorkshire company on 2nd March 1933 signed an agreement with Fawdon to purchase all the shares at the rate of 27s6d per £1 share. A total of £4416 5s was paid, £4166 5s for the shares and £250 to J.J.Berry for his work in the purchase. For the subsequent redistribution, the service was divided into two. The Newcastle-Leeds section was transferred to the Limited Stop Pool, and the Leeds-Coventry section to the Yorkshire Services Pool. The purchase price was to be levied one third from the Limited Stop Pool and two thirds from the Yorkshire Services Pool. The two amounts were then to be subdivided amongst the members of each Pool as their individual cost of the purchase. When the licences on Fawdon vehicles expired on 24th March 1933 they were not renewed, and the company applied to the Traffic Commissioners for a "Permit to Hire", which was granted to them. In the period 25th March to 12th April 1933 the service was operated by Northern on hire to Fawdon. However, as West Yorkshire and Yorkshire WD were the only members of both Pools, they took over the running of the service from 13th April 1933. The licences were to remain in the name of Fawdon for over 25 years, but by the time they applied for a modification on 20th May 1933, the firm's address had become 117 Queen Street, Bensham, Gateshead. This of course was Northern's head office.

14. 1933 - Takeover of Leeds & Newcastle and of Tyne & Mersey

As we saw above, when the United company came to the conference table on 2nd May 1933,

it was able to offer a substantial contribution to the Pool network, in marked contrast to its position at the conference of November 1930. The agreement to purchase the assets and goodwill of the Leeds & Newcastle company had been signed on 11th April. United would keep the local services in the Northallerton area along with a due proportion of the vehicles, but would offer to the Pool the Newcastle - Leeds and Middlesbrough - Northallerton services. The purchase took effect on 1st August 1933 as described below. On that date three Gilford and two Tilling-Stevens vehicles were acquired by United, and the others passed jointly to the Pool partners and were re-sold on their behalf.

The conference of 2nd May 1933 had resolved to purchase the Tyne & Mersey company which, as we saw above in section 11, was operating a once daily service between Newcastle and Liverpool via Leeds and Bradford, with a Redcar - Darlington feeder. Its owners were obviously willing to sell, because they signed the purchase agreement with Northern only two weeks later, on 16th May. Applications were then made in the names of North Western, Northern, United, West Yorkshire, Yorkshire WD and Lancashire United for licences to take over this service without any amendments to it. This was granted on 10th October 1933 in the North Western TA and around that date in the other areas, and the purchase agreement took effect on 18th. United thereby became a Pool member from 18th October 1933, but initially this was only in respect of the ex-Tyne & Mersey service, which remained separately licensed from the other Pool services. Indeed, it was to retain its separate licence not only until operation via Bradford ceased in 1962 but, in revised form, to the end of the Pool's existence. The three Tyne & Mersey coaches did not join any of the partners' fleets, but were re-sold by Northern on behalf of the Pool.

15. 1933-34 - United and the Licensing Struggles

The main application to introduce a new service between Liverpool and Middlesbrough (extended to Redcar in summer) was refused by the Commissioners, as was the admission of United as a joint operator on the other Newcastle services. The Commissioners would not allow through bookings to continue, and also imposed a duplication restriction on the service. The final blow came from the North

West Yorkshire's **640** (**DWU138**) was in the last year of its full coaching cream livery when photographed *(upper)* in Durham bus station on 19th April 1953. For the 1954 season the class was painted red. It was this type of coach which inspired the drawing on the timetable leaflet reproduced on our back cover. The same cream coach livery graced the 1950 Bristol L6B *(lower)* which had a clear 'family resemblance' to the L6G. West Yorkshire's **661** (**JWU890**) had arrived at the Newcastle, Haymarket, terminus on 1st July 1953. *(Both: D S Burnicle)*

Western TC who would grant only single fares on the fare table, not returns. The Pool could not operate adequately under these restrictions, so appeals were lodged against the decisions.

As the Pool had purchased the agreed ex-LNOC services from United, it was decided that these should continue to be operated by United on the Pool's behalf, with United receiving the Pool mileage rate. It was clearly intended to be a short term expedient, but the licensing difficulties extended that term considerably. United took over the LNOC services on 1st August 1933. The Newcastle - Leeds service was numbered 66 in its Durham Area series, and continued to operate via Neville's Cross and also via Northallerton and Thirsk. It thus differed from the main Pool services which ran via Durham city, and via Scotch Corner and Catterick Village. Between Thirsk and Ripon the LNOC had used the main A61 road via Baldersby, and when United took over they diverted the ex-Redwing service 60 this way too, and incorporated Dishforth in the rural service 19 mentioned in section 12 above. The Middlesbrough, Stockton and Northallerton service was numbered 59. As a stage carriage service it was slower than the United and West Yorkshire joint ex-Redwing express service 60 to Leeds. Northbound (but not southbound) times between Leeds and Northallerton were evenly spaced, with the 60 leaving Leeds on the odd hour, and the 66 on the even hour. Conversely southbound (but not northbound) journeys between Middlesbrough and Northallerton were evenly spaced, with the 59 leaving Middlesbrough on the odd hour, and the 60 on the even hour. The two ex-LNOC services (59 and 66) had originally been designed to connect at Northallerton, but under United's auspices this only applied to northbound journeys, and probably without through fares. The effect was an hourly service from Leeds to Middlesbrough but only two-hourly vice versa.

The appeals were heard on 21st-23rd June 1934 and the decision was given on 20th September 1934 by the Minister of Transport. There had been 25 appeals and the report ran to 21 pages. It overruled the Traffic Commissioners on nearly every point. It granted the Liverpool - Redcar service. The proposal for United to join the Pool was judged to be in the public interest, as were the through bookings on to connecting services. The Minister noted the lack of any evidence that the Road Service Licences (Appeal) Orders (54,55) of 1933 regarding duplication restrictions should be applied to these licences, so he again overruled the Commissioners. He might have changed his mind if he had known that on Saturday 18th August 1934 138 duplicate vehicles were operated on the Pool services. Lastly, as no discussions had taken place with the operators regarding the abolition of return fares, he again overruled the North Western TC. The LNER had also appealed against certain fares, but the Minister disallowed their appeal.

16. 1934 - Success and Expansion

The way was now open to revise the Pool, and important changes came into effect on 21st October 1934. The Liverpool - Hull service was to be withdrawn on 9th December. However the timings between Liverpool and Leeds were now to be used for the Middlesbrough service, so East Yorkshire operated a shuttle service between Leeds and Hull from 21st October to 9th December, receiving the average Pool rate for the miles run. After this, East Yorkshire was no longer a Pool member. United withdrew the ex-LNOC service 66, which was incorporated in the new licences, as was the Redcar - Leeds service 60 of United and West Yorkshire. Crosville finally gave up their Liverpool - Manchester licences, surrendering by 17th November 1934. It was agreed that after 9th December through bookings would be made to Hull via the much slower West Yorkshire and East Yorkshire joint stage carriage service from Leeds via York. They received 4s6d, which was half the return fare, for each passenger carried who held a Limited Stop return ticket.

During this time Red & White Motor Services of Chepstow had applied in October 1933 for a service between Liverpool and Manchester via the newly opened A580 East Lancashire Road. The application was later withdrawn, after Red & White had reached agreement with Ribble and Crosville for the takeover of their other express services in the Liverpool area.

17. 1935 - Opposition and Restrictions

In the early period licences were granted for only a year and no sooner had the appeal decision been received than renewal applications had to be made. The railways objected on the grounds that the services were of a long distance nature, and unlimited duplication resulted in wasteful competition with the railway services already provided. The

At the opposite end of the scale when it came to helpful destination blinds was the "Limited Stop" display without any place names at all. An example (upper) from the United fleet was **LTO65** (**EHN965**), which was photographed in Wellington Street, Leeds, just about to turn into the coach station. It was probably working a duplicate from Darlington circa 1949. Similar coaches based at Middlesbrough depot were properly equipped, particularly after their 1951 refurbishment. In this latter-day condition, United's **LLE17** (**EHN968**) of 1939 was photographed (lower) in the market place at Thirsk circa 1957. The destination display "Leeds, Northallerton, Harrogate" reflected the post-Suez period when fewer Middlesbrough departures were scheduled to run through to Liverpool, with or without a change of coach at Leeds. *(PB Collection; R F Mack Collection)*

hearing took place at Newcastle on 12th December 1934, when a reserved decision was given enabling the Northern TA to consult with the other two areas. The Commissioners were aware that the Pool operators had won one appeal on duplication, but it still took them until 25th March 1935 to decide. They stated that the number of through journeys between Liverpool and Newcastle operated by the railways was insufficient to be regarded as one of the trunk services that required protection against duplication. Furthermore they did not think that the low percentage of through passengers carried by the road services justified the limitation of duplication specified in the Minister's Orders 54 and 55 of 1933.

Yorkshire TA still managed to be different, and when the backings for the 1935 season were received, the facility of through bookings between the Pool and the Leeds - Hull stage carriage service had been deleted. The Commissioners stated that as only one operator (West Yorkshire) held a licence for both routes, they were not in a position to grant the other six operators through fares over sections of route which they were not licensed to operate. They therefore did not propose to let the West Yorkshire and East Yorkshire joint stage service have through fares in view of the joint operation of the Liverpool part of the service.

18. Services and Mileages

The Pool had now settled into a regular pattern:-

1) Liverpool - Newcastle via Altrincham and Dewsbury, 2-hourly;
2) Leeds - Newcastle alternately with 1, 2-hourly;
3) Liverpool - Middlesbrough (Redcar seasonal) via Eccles and Liversedge, 2-hourly;
4) Newcastle - Liverpool via Bradford, once daily & return;
5) Newcastle - Leeds (to Coventry), Fawdon Service, once daily & return; and
6) Liverpool - Manchester via Altrincham or Eccles (Summer SSuBH), hourly.

The fares on the ex-Tyne & Mersey service (no.4) were revised in 1935, to bring them into line with the other Pool fares. After this, with the exception of the 1939-45 war years, this pattern of operation continued until the Suez crisis in the 'fifties. Despite fairly frequent minor timetable variations, the general prewar pattern was that this service via Bradford was superimposed on the two-hourly structure. Postwar, it was mostly absorbed into the two-hourly structure, but not entirely. For example, at some periods an extra Leeds-Manchester journey was operated simultaneously via Dewsbury.

The revised services brought about a new mileage agreement which meant that the Pool was broken up into sections for mileage only, the revenue paid to each member being based on the mileage run. This worked out as follows:-

Liverpool - Newcastle via Bradford (ex-Tyne & Mersey):-
Lancashire United 10.8%
North Western 27.8%
United 10.4%
Northern, West Yorkshire, Yorkshire WD all 17%.

Newcastle - Leeds (Fawdon):-
North Western, Northern, West Yorkshire, Yorkshire WD all 25%

Newcastle - Leeds only (not the through timings from Manchester):-
North Western, Northern, United, West Yorkshire, Yorkshire WD, all 20%

Manchester - Leeds - Newcastle (all services not shown above):-
North Western, Northern, West Yorkshire, Yorkshire WD, all 25%

Manchester - Liverpool (all services except ex-Tyne & Mersey):-
North Western, Lancashire United, both 50%

Middlesbrough - Leeds (Redcar in summer):-
United 66.67%, West Yorkshire 33.33%

The company with the highest Pool mileage entitlement was North Western with 25.1%, and Lancashire United the lowest with 11.7%. West Yorkshire had 20.5%, United 15.7%, while Northern and Yorkshire WD both had 13.5%. The fact that LUT had no mileage entitlement north of Manchester, except for the ex-Tyne & Mersey, was due to their refusal to allow the other companies any percentage on their Manchester-Liverpool section. Their claim on the service via Bradford was because it entered Liverpool via Eccles which was LUT territory.

On alternate summer Saturdays the through coach from Lowestoft on the Limited Stop timings left an Eastern Counties vehicle at Middlesbrough depot for the following week, although the crews had changed over half way. In theory it was not meant to be used by United during the week, but if there was nothing else available, out it went. After all, the depot was short of the bus which was theoretically holed up at Lowestoft but could often be seen in London! It was a Thursday when **LE699** (**KNG699**) was photographed *(upper)* behind Middlesbrough bus station on 29th July 1954, the ECOC "Relief" destination being of the usual practical use to prospective passengers. On another occasion *(lower)*, this time circa 1958, Eastern Counties sent **DS981** (**EX6350**), a 1949 Dennis Lancet, which no doubt entertained both United's staff and passengers. *(D S Burnicle, Geoffrey Holt)*

This mileage agreement did not mean that LUT could not operate north of Manchester, because they ran off the mileage not operated by them on the Liverpool - Manchester section due to the through running of the other operators. For instance, on 6th May 1935 LUT took over from North Western the 8.05am Manchester - Newcastle and the 4.20pm Newcastle - Manchester. On 11th August they took over from United the 8.10am Darlington - Liverpool and the 4.05pm Liverpool - Darlington, while on 1st September they operated the 7.15am Leeds - Liverpool and the 12.05pm Liverpool - Newcastle for North Western, all to run off their accumulated mileage. The running could be for a day, or even a few weeks, depending on the mileage to be run. This was of course common to all the operators who accumulated mileage for one reason or another. For example, the most usual for North Western was the Fawdon mileage, which mounted up because they did not operate on that service. This meant running some of either West Yorkshire or Yorkshire WD entitlement on the other routes to balance. Regular patterns developed which could confuse the observer. One of your authors has a memory of the daily operation of Lancashire United to Middlesbrough in the period 1954-56. Another careful north-eastern observer of many years cannot recall United ever working the Leeds - Newcastle section, although in fact summer Saturdays saw the company providing vehicles between Darlington and Leeds. Indeed, at peak periods you could expect to see any of the operators on any part of the service

19. How the Pool Worked

Now that the Pool had settled down, we can take the opportunity to see how it worked. The Pool was managed by meetings between all the general managers, who then passed matters to their traffic managers. These subsequently reported back to their general managers. It might have been long winded, but seemed to work. Any business of importance occurring between meetings was settled by correspondence.

The Limited Stop Pool operated differently from the Associated Motorways, which held the Road Service licences in its own name and then listed the joint operators or members. In the case of the Pool, each operator held its own licences, with the condition that they were to be operated jointly with the other licence holders. Four licences were held by each of the Pool partners,

making a total of 24 altogether. Apart from the Liverpool-Redcar service which was stage carriage, the others were all express. There were also the summer weekend extra Manchester - Liverpool services, which were licensed to North Western and Lancashire United only, but were included in the Pool mileage reckoning. The four were:-

Newcastle - Liverpool via Bradford and Eccles
Liverpool - Redcar via Eccles and Liversedge
Liverpool - Newcastle via Altrincham and Dewsbury
Liverpool - Newcastle via Eccles and Liversedge.

The last licence was not a through service. It consisted of short workings between Liverpool and Manchester, Liverpool and Leeds, and Leeds and Newcastle, operating on various days of the week and season, and none of them connected. In 1949 each operator's licence for these workings was surrendered. The timings were transferred to the other Newcastle or the Middlesbrough licences. (The Redcar summer extension did not operate postwar). At the beginning each operator was responsible for renewing its own licences, but errors occurred. It was therefore decided that North Western should prepare all applications for the North Western TA, while West Yorkshire dealt with the Yorkshire TA, and Northern with the Northern TA. These companies represented the Pool operators in the respective traffic courts where necessary. Northern also acted as accountants for the Pool, whilst West Yorkshire dealt with publicity and timetables, and Yorkshire WD saw to ticket supplies. Certain expenses were charged against the Pool services for publicity, Traffic Commissioners, station charges, and drivers' and conductors' lodgings and meals. The reconciliation of the amount to be debited or credited to each company was obtained by calculating and comparing the total receipts per car mile, each company's mileage, and the actual receipts of that company.

20. 1934-37 - Thirsk - Northallerton Local Fares

When the Liverpool - Middlesbrough service was introduced on 21st October 1934 and United had accordingly withdrawn its 60 and 66 services, there were no intermediate fares for

The two buses shown here at Lower Mosley Street, Manchester, could be described as good vehicles, but over-stretched as far as passenger comfort went. Lancashire United's **191** (**KTB104**) was slightly the better in its seating, and treated the passenger to the distinctive Guy 'whistle' that made the journey over the Pennines so memorable. United's **BB17** (**LHN561**) had the powerful Bristol engine in the L6B chassis, which would perhaps make possible an extra tea break, as sometimes happened. In these scenes, 191 (upper) was terminating at Manchester and BB17 (lower) was about to depart for Middlesbrough. *(R.F.Mack Collection; Keith Healey)*

stages between Thirsk and Northallerton. The ex-LNOC 59 Middlesbrough, Stockton, Yarm and Northallerton service had been withdrawn previously, replaced on 1st March 1934 by the ex-Blumer's Middlesbrough, Stokesley, Osmotherley and Northallerton service. This also took the number 59, which it retained until 1967. A licence to extend it from Northallerton to Thirsk to meet the local demand was granted on 24th November 1934, but the extension was not justified by results. By February 1936 it was reduced to MSO; Monday was market day in Thirsk. This left the Pool services with a minimum fare of 1s between the two points, whereas the stage carriage fare had been 9d and with intermediate stages too. Complaints were received by the Northern Traffic Commissioners about this increase. The Pool then made application for a panel of fares to be inserted into the table, available only between Thirsk and Northallerton, with fares as low as 1d. This was granted. It created an anomaly in fares whereby passengers travelling from, say, Manchester to Northallerton could by rebooking at Thirsk obtain a cheaper fare than by booking through. The Pool then applied for a new fare table which would remove this anomaly.

In the Northern TA the railway companies objected to the fare revisions. In the primary area, the North Western TC granted the revisions because no objections were received. However the backing applications to Yorkshire TA and Northern TA were refused. The same procedure was followed for the 1937 renewals, but this time Yorkshire TA and North Western TA granted the revisions, though Northern TA again refused. This was appealed against, the Minister upholding the Northern TA's decision. On receiving the Minister's decision the North Western TC immediately varied their original grant and refused the revisions in light of the appeal. This left Yorkshire TA as usual the odd one out, granting the revisions. It resulted in two more appeals, LNER against Yorkshire TA for granting the Pool's application, and the Pool members against the North Western TA for refusing the application. The main reasoning for the Pool was "that it was not in the public interest, that if one member of the public knew of the facilities for obtaining a cheaper fare by double booking, that this information should be withheld from other members of the public. It is not reasonable that two people should travel between the same two points at different fares, and a system which allows such a state of things savours of duplicity." Unfortunately the Pool in this instance did not win. The railways won their appeal over the Yorkshire TA decision, so the double booking anomaly remained.

21. Connecting Services

As the Pool operated cross-country it was natural that connecting facilities were advertised. Through bookings were available including:-

Liverpool - Manchester - Nottingham
Birmingham - Manchester - Huddersfield
Birmingham - Manchester - Liverpool
Potteries - Manchester - Liverpool
Potteries - Manchester - Newcastle
Leeds - Newcastle - Edinburgh
Newcastle - Manchester - North Wales.

The Pool granted 7.5% commission to operators such as Potteries Motor Traction and Midland Red (BMMO) for pre-booked passengers. These arrangements were natural successors to the connections at Leeds established by Progress Motors and LNOC which had even continued during winter 1933 when both firms had been sold to the associated companies.

22. Bus Stations

As we have noted already, the bus stations at Lower Mosley Street, Manchester, and Wellington Street, Leeds, were of central importance to the successful operation of the Pool services. By contrast, terminal arrangements in Liverpool were always unsatisfactory.

In Newcastle, Northern's bus station in Worswick Street had been used from the beginning. This was on a sloping site, and wooden chocks were used as an aid to safety. The Tyne & Mersey ('Overland') and Leeds & Newcastle companies had operated from Marlborough Crescent bus station, close to the Central railway station. Latterly, probably from April 1932, Tyne & Mersey had extended to the more northerly Haymarket bus station, giving connections with services to the north. When United took over the LNOC service, this too was transferred to Haymarket. The Pool continued to use Haymarket for the 'Overland' service, but all its other journeys still terminated at Worswick Street until United joined the Pool proper in October 1934. From then until the end of the Pool, both Haymarket and Worswick

The Tyne - Tees - Mersey services were extremely heavily duplicated in the summer peak periods but the Liverpool terminus was simply a bus stop in the street at Mount Pleasant outside the LUT office. The 1949 move to the inconvenient Russell Street was occasioned by the ending of the company's lease on the office, for which a temporary replacement was erected on the new site. In this picture United's **BBE12** (**NHN125**), a 33-seat Bristol LL6B, was loading at Russell Street for Middlesbrough. *(Ribble Enthusiasts)*

A longer Bristol L-series chassis was also used by West Yorkshire as the basis of a coach. In this case the 35-seat vehicle was **CBW12** in the fleet (**JYG741**), an LWL6B. It displayed a "Llandudno" label for the summer Saturday linked services, but on this occasion the coach was not required to go beyond Manchester. It was therefore parked at the nearby East Street coach station, where it was photographed, and would be sent back to Yorkshire as and when required. *(Keith Healey)*

Street were served, but not Marlborough Crescent.

The only other bus stations used by the Pool from the beginning were Altrincham, Durham and Middlesbrough (Exchange). Everywhere else the Pool services had initially picked up at designated bus stops in the street. This situation remained to the end in Liverpool, Warrington, Huddersfield and Stockton, but in various other places bus stations were built in due course. In Darlington, long distance services were using a stance in Grange Road from 1927 but by 1932 the Pool services were using the rather primitive bus station in the Leadyard. The stations built at Dewsbury and Eccles in 1932 and 1939 came into use during and following major tramway abandonments. Another move in the wake of a tramway route closure was at Huddersfield in 1935. The Pool services were transferred from the Kirkgate main thoroughfare into Venn Street, an adjacent side street where Yorkshire WD had a booking office until the mid-1950s.

Bradford (Chester Street) bus station opened in February 1936, and Northallerton in June of the same year. In Middlesbrough, services moved from the Exchange to United's own new bus station in Newport Road in October 1937. The following month saw West Yorkshire open Vicar Lane bus station in Leeds, although the Pool services only stopped outside it, a facility omitted after the war but restored by April 1950. Other new stations were opened in Harrogate and Redcar in July 1938. In what might be termed the opposite direction, the Darlington timing point by June 1948 was a street stance in Feethams instead of the Leadyard bus station. Postwar developments included new bus stations at Ripon in May 1951, Darlington in September 1961 and Oldham, Clegg Street, in May 1966.

The use of bus stations by buses on the Pool services involved the payment of standage charges. Full accounts consisting of the rates for each station, and the number of departures made, were included in the Pool's internal correspondence, and the costs divided out appropriately. In some circumstances, conductors had to issue standage vouchers to bus station officials as part of the owner's system of record keeping.

23. 1938-39 - Before the War

In 1938 the Pool was granted its application to pick up and set down passengers at Barton Airport, the original Manchester Airport. This was situated on the north side of the A57 between Irlam and Eccles, and had opened on 1st January 1930. It was ironic that the limitations of the Barton site had led to the opening of the new Manchester Airport at Ringway in June 1938, so that the Pool's facility to stop at Barton came rather late in the day. Nevertheless, Barton Airport remained an additional request stop until the end of the Pool. Application was also made to extend the extra hourly Manchester - Liverpool service to operate over Easter weekend and on the Friday following Whit Monday. This was granted in December, in time for the 1939 season.

That summer was a time of anxious expectancy, and not without cause. The Second World War commenced on 3rd September 1939, and nothing was ever the same again, including buses. The Pool services were reduced immediately. Subsequent complete withdrawal of the Limited Stop took place after operation on Sunday 9th June 1940, by order of the Regional Transport Commissioner. The Fawdon service between Newcastle and Coventry survived until 20th July 1941, when it too was ordered to stop. Reinstatement was of course quite unpredictable, as no one knew how long the war would last.

24. 1940-45 - Wartime Exigencies

In the absence of the Limited Stop services during the war, journeys had to be made by local services, changing where necessary along the line of route. This echoed the situation in the early stages of bus service development twenty years before, particularly as there were some unexpected gaps caused by other route withdrawals. There seems to have been no service between Northallerton and Thirsk. United introduced a new service, numbered 28, between Darlington, Catterick and Ripon. Passengers by road from Middlesbrough and Stockton were directed to travel this way to reach Harrogate and Leeds. It was also the only way, albeit very circuitous, for them to reach Thirsk by bus. North Western's Oldham-Huddersfield service ceased too, although in this case the parallel Hanson service kept running.

25. 1946-49 - Starting Up Again

The first part of the Pool's activities to recommence was the Fawdon service. The competing Hall Bros service between South

The inclusion of Darlington on the destination display on West Yorkshire's **658** (**FWX809**) at Derby makes clear that this coach was operating the Fawdon Bus Company's route from Newcastle. The date was June 1954, several years before the Fawdon company's licences were transferred to the actual operating companies. *(G H F Atkins)*

In what we now see as a wonderful period view at Wellington Street, Leeds, Northern's AEC-Beadle **1483** (**DCN83**) was operating through to Liverpool. Duplication was provided by **1315** (**HD5823**), one of Northern's numerous ex-Yorkshire WD TS7 vehicles, and North Western's **154** (**CDB154**), a Bristol L5G. The date was April 1955. *(G H F Atkins)*

Shields, Doncaster and Coventry restarted in 1946, and the Fawdon service did likewise on 20th July, exactly five years after ceasing for the duration. Meanwhile, in March 1946 applications were lodged for permits to recommence the Liverpool services. A timetable was forwarded to the Traffic Commissioners at the end of June, followed by an amendment in September. A further application was made to increase all fares except between Ripon and Middlesbrough. These applications were approved, and the services recommenced on 6th October. All passengers were now required to change at Leeds, though duplicate vehicles were run across Leeds. Four days beforehand, on 2nd October 1946, the North Western Oldham - Huddersfield service had been restored on a limited basis. All Manchester - Leeds journeys (except the ex-Tyne & Mersey service via Bradford) now ran via Mirfield and Dewsbury. The Liversedge variation, which simply followed the main A62 road between Huddersfield and Leeds, was not restored. For the summer season in 1947, the Limited Stop crew information book issued in June showed details of operation through to Redcar.

However, the seasonal Middlesbrough-Redcar section was not operated that year, and was in fact never reinstated after the war.

From Monday 11th April 1949, the picking up point at Liverpool was moved from Mount Pleasant at the insistence of the police. The new terminus was in Russell Street, a rather inconvenient site to the rear of Lime Street station. On 25th October 1949 the North Western TA authorised the use of lowbridge double deckers on duplicate workings between Manchester and Liverpool. The height was specified as "not exceeding 13ft 3½ins". In the same year the 6 and 12 month contract rates on the Middlesbrough-Harrogate section were withdrawn, though the 1, 2 and 3 month rates remained. An additional return journey was introduced at weekends between Middlesbrough and Northallerton for visitors to Northallerton Hospital. The outward journey was SO but the return journey was operated SSu. In July 1952 application was made to extend these journeys to the hospital, even though it was just behind the bus station. The problem was that for the return journey the bus was loading up with ordinary passengers before the visitors arrived from the hospital.

LIVERPOOL—ECCLES—MANCHESTER—DEWSBURY—LEEDS—MIDDLESBROUGH

DAILY

		am	am	am	am	am	pm	pm			a m	am	pm	pm	pm	pm	pm
LIVERPOOL (Russell Street)	dep.			7 55	9 55	1155	1 55		MIDDLESBRO' (Newport Road) dep.	8 35	1035	1235	2 35	5 50		7 50
Prescot (Hope and Anchor)	"		8 25	1025	1225	2 25		STOCKTON (United Office, High St.)	8 48	1048	1248	2 48	6 3		8 3
Warrington (Bridgefoot)	"		8 51	1051	1251	2 51		Yarm (Market Place)	8 59	1059	1259	2 59	6 14		8 14
Irlam (Station)			9 9	11 9	1 9	3 9		Crathorne	9 9	11 9	1 9	3 9	6 24		8 24
ECCLES (Bus Station)	"		9 25	1125	1 25	3 25		Clack Lane Ends	9 26	1126	1 26	3 26	6 41		8 41
Manchester (Lower Mosley St.) arr.			9 43	1143	1 43	3 43		NORTHALLERTON (Bus Stn.)	9 41	1141	1 41	3 41	6 56		8 56
MANCHESTER (L'w'r Mosley St.) dep.		7†43	9 43	1143	1 43	3 43		THIRSK (Royal Oak)	10 5	12 52	5 4	5 7 20		9 20
Oldham (Greaves St. G.P.O.)	"	8†15	1015	1215	2 15	4 15		Thirsk (Market Place)	10†20	1220	2 20	4 20	7 20		9 20
Uppermill (Commercial Hotel)	"	8†30	1030	1230	2 30	4 30		York (Rougier Street)	arr. 11 30	1 27	3 27	5 27	8 24		1027
Marsden (New Inn)	"	8†47	1047	1247	2 47	4 47		Ripon (Bus Station)	dep. 10 32	1232	2 32	4 32	7 47	755	9 47
HUDDERSFIELD (Venn Street)	"	9†	6 11	61	63	65	6	HARROGATE (Bus Station)	"	11 0	1 03	3 05	0		823	1015
Mirfield (Ing Grove Park)	"	9†21	1121	1 21	3 21	5 21		Harewood (Harewood Arms)	"	11 20	1 20	3 20	5 20		843	
DEWSBURY (Bus Station)	"	9†30	1130	1 30	3 30	5 30		LEEDS (Wellington St. Bus Stn.) arr.	11 43	1 43	3 43	5 43		9 6	
LEEDS (Wellington St. Bus Stn.) arr.		9†55	1155	1 55	3 55	5 55									
									LEEDS (Wellington St. Bus Stn.) dep.	12 25	2 25	4 25	6 25			
LEEDS (Wellington St. Bus Stn.)	dep.	8 35	1035	1235	2 35	4 35	6 35	DEWSBURY (Bus Station)	12 50	2 50	4 50	6 50			
Harewood (Harewood Arms)	"	8 58	1058	1258	2 58	4 58	6 58	Mirfield (Ing Grove Park)	12 59	2 59	4 59	6 59			
HARROGATE (Bus Station)	"	9 18	1118	1 18	3 18	5 18	7 18	HUDDERSFIELD (Venn Street)	1 14	3 14	5 14	7 14			
Ripon (Bus Station)	"	9 46	1146	1 46	3 46	5 46	7 46	7 55	Marsden (New Inn)	1 20	3 20	5 20	843			
THIRSK (Royal Oak)	arr.	1013	1213	2 13	4 13	6 13	8 22	Uppermill (Commercial Hotel)	1 50	3 50	5 50	7 50			
York (Rougier Street)	dep.	9†	10	11	10	1	10 3	10	7S10	Oldham (Greaves Street G.P.O.)	2 54	56	58	5			
Thirsk (Market Place)	arr.	1017	1214	2 14	4 14		8S14	Manchester (Lower Mosley Street) arr.	2 37	4 37	6 37	8 37			
THIRSK (Royal Oak)	dep.	1017	1217	2 17	4 17	6 17	8 25	MANCHESTER (L'w'r Mosley St.) dep.	2 37	4 37	6 37	8 37			
NORTHALLERTON (Bus Stn.)	"	1040	1240	2 40	4 40	6 40	8 48	ECCLES (Bus Station)	2 55	4 55	6 55	8 55			
Clack Lane Ends	"	1055	1255	2 55	4 55	6 55	9 3	Irlam (Station)	3 11	5 11	7 11	9 11			
Crathorne	"	1112	1 12	3 12	5 12	7 12	9 20	Warrington (Bridgefoot)	3 20	5 20	7 20	843			
Yarm (Market Place)	"	1122	2 22	3 22	5 22	7 22	9 30	Prescott (opp. Westminster Bank)	3 29	5 29	7 29	9 29			
STOCKTON (United Office, High St.)	"	1133	1 33	3 33	5 33	7 33	9 41	LIVERPOOL (Russell Street) arr.	3 55	5 55	7 55	9 55			
MIDDLESBRO' (Newport Road)	arr.	1146	1 46	3 46	5 46	7 46	9 54	LIVERPOOL (Russell Street) ... arr.	4 25	6 25	8 25	1025			

†—Not Sunday   S—Saturday only

Additional journeys Saturday only : Dep. Middlesbrough 11·55 am, arr. Northallerton (Hospital) 1·1 pm

Additional journeys Saturdays and Sundays only :—Dep. Northallerton (Hospital) 4·0 pm, arr. Middlesbrough 5-6 pm

This example of the Liverpool to Middlesbrough timetable dates from 20th May 1954

Another Northern AEC-Beadle was **1485** (**DCN85**) *(upper)*, an attractive coach which offered a comfortable journey to "Manchester via Leeds, Dewsbury, Limited Stop Service". A further addition to the wide variety of vehicles to be found on the Tyne - Tees - Mersey services was Yorkshire WD's **772** (**AHD51**) *(lower)*, a 1954 Plaxton-bodied Bedford. It had been acquired with the business of Braggs Motors, and the Newcastle destination was shown on the inevitable paper label. Both pictures were taken at Feethams, Darlington, in August 1960. *(R A Stone)*

26. On the Road with the Limited Stop

Passengers' attitudes to the service depended on the road staff who looked after them. Letters in the "Nor Wester" staff magazine illustrated the point. One complained of having to wait an hour and a half in the queue at Liverpool with a hundred other people, and being moved about so often that the place was in complete chaos. When they were finally boarding a bus the conductor warned them, "If you're not careful I will throw the lot of you off". This he did when he found eight passengers with Lancashire United tickets for the 32 service via St.Helens to Manchester. He gave them no option to pay, and left them at the roadside. By then the time was 10.15pm, and he returned to Liverpool to inform the office of what he had done. In contrast, a couple who travelled from Liverpool to Newcastle and return, with changes at Manchester and Leeds, had nothing but praise for the conductors who were most helpful and courteous whether from Northern, West Yorkshire or North Western.

The principal refreshment stop for the Liverpool services was Leeds, Wellington Street. The Fawdon service stopped variously at Boroughbridge, Leeds, Barnsley and Chesterfield over the years, but between Ripon and Darlington both services also had a short break at Catterick until 1950. Inadequate facilites and poor service led to a change to Jock's Café at Leeming as from 30th April 1950. The passengers, crews and operating companies loved it, but elsewhere feathers were ruffled. It seems that the Catterick café had recently changed hands after a long period of decline, and the new owner had probably paid a good price on the basis of guaranteed traffic, but too late. Letters to the press, rumblings by members of Richmond R.D.C., and pressure from the café owner had all to be handled by United's traffic manager, the appropriately named H.G.Baker. United was here the local Pool operator, yet it is likely that a United bus hardly ever used the premises from one end of the year to the other! In the event, the operators stayed with the Leeming café until after the village was by-passed and the Leeming Motel came into use in 1962.

The extensive use of ordinary service buses by all the operators, especially on summer Saturdays in the postwar period, was notorious. The Limited Stop was perhaps the least prestigious of the various companies' long distance services. Many passengers made comparatively short journeys, but that still meant two or three hours which, for example, was a very long time to sit on one of Northern's 38-seat Guy Arabs designed for a typical journey of 15 to 20 minutes. As for passengers with luggage, the prospect hardly bears thinking about. Summer Saturdays must have been the only experience of the Limited Stop for most passengers, many of whom probably said "Never again", thus contributing in due course to the decline. This is not to say that the companies were in a position to do anything about it. They had not enough coaches to go round. Nevertheless, in another context, Horace Bottomley, the general manager of Ribble, said in 1960 that "it has been amply demonstrated that joint service interests are secondary to the partners' own interests".

Another aspect of being on the road was that of the companies' staffs. The services were so intensive, and had to cope with such huge surges of demand in the peak season, that local crews could be sent off into strange territory at a moment's notice. The Crews' Instruction Book was designed to cope with these situations, providing always that a copy was to hand. It was one of those documents which used the strangely formal term "Northern Pool", and the 1966 edition ran to 40 pages without including timetables, faretables, or anything about the Coventry service. It included full route details, how to get to and from the various garages, acres of instructions about tickets, maps of all the town centres and - at the beginning! - which depot to telephone if you broke down. This list contained a few surprises, because breakdown coverage was arranged on a practical basis which sometimes differed from the companies' agreed operating territories listed above in section 9. Thus Yorkshire WD provided cover as far as Marsden, in North Western's territory, West Yorkshire south from Leeds as far as Tingley Cross Roads, and Northern as far south as Ferryhill. United's Durham depot was not listed, although the route almost passed the door, but Richmond depot covered a section of the Great North Road. The LUT depot at Atherton covered not only the Eccles section between Manchester and Warrington, but also the route between Warrington and Liverpool. No doubt a rescue job would be passed on to the company's garage in Bentley Road, Liverpool, if need be. The ticket instructions showed the abbreviations to be used if issuing a written ticket. Most of them were obvious enough, but "S/FORD" meant

Yorkshire WD also had a dozen Beadle-bodied coaches with Commer TS3 running units which were not widely found elsewhere. They seated 41 and dated from 1957. In this scene at Wellington Street, Leeds, **778** (**CHD363**) was waiting to depart for Liverpool. *(Photobus)*

A new era dawned with the introduction of underfloor-engined vehicles, but this often meant no more than that they had a greater capacity. A case in point was Northern's **1573** (**DCN873**), a Leyland 44-seater bus bound for Liverpool and seen just arriving at Wellington Street, Leeds. It carried the attractive original maroon livery, and the tramlines reveal that the view dates from 1954-57. *(PB collection)*

Stretford, not Salford, which city did not have a fare stage at all. You had to be booked from Manchester westbound and Eccles eastbound. Incidentally, the Salford request stop was on Regent Road at Cross Lane, the site of the renowned 'grand union' tramway junction now awaiting eventual reassembly at the National Tramway Museum at Crich. Another potentially confusing abbreviation was "D/BY" for Dewsbury, not Derby on the Fawdon service. Why not "D/BURY"? After all, there was space for "HAREWOOD" which had to be written in full. Indeed, the longest abbreviation was "T/LE/BEANS" for Thornton-le-Beans (between Thirsk and Northallerton), and the shortest, as you might have expected, was "M/C" for Manchester.

27. 1951-54 - The Development of Holiday Traffic

In 1951 the Pool requested permission to operate duplicate vehicles out of Leeds northwards from 6.00am on summer Saturdays, and to continue to operate them until the first authorised time of departure, which was 8.35am. This was granted on 18th May in time for the 1951 season. Anybody who has been to Wellington Street at Leeds will appreciate the problem of passengers arriving well before departure times and thereby causing congestion. 1951 saw also the commencement of through running of service cars between Liverpool and Newcastle. However, it only involved Northern and North Western, who changed their crews over at Leeds. They were both insured by the BET Federation, so drivers were covered for both companies' vehicles. Other companies still operated duplicates across Leeds, and provided crew lodgings at the far end where necessary. Through bookings to North Wales via Manchester were also recommenced in 1951 after being suspended since 1939. Also in 1951, West Yorkshire were involved with the provision of a through coach between Newcastle and Keighley, and at the end of the season proposals were being examined for through running between Blackpool and Newcastle via Leeds. Another proposal at that time was for the joint Ribble and West Yorkshire service between Liverpool and Scarborough via Bolton and Leeds to accept Limited Stop passengers if space was available.

Ill feeling between the West Yorkshire and Yorkshire WD companies after the 1951 season rumbled on into the 1952 summer season. The problem was the provision of sufficient inspectors to control traffic at Wellington Street, Leeds, at busy times. Yorkshire WD appeared to take the view that it was not their bus station, whereas West Yorkshire was having to supervise the use of other sites nearby to accommodate its own services to Whitby, Scarborough, Bridlington and Blackpool because Wellington Street was fully occupied with huge Limited Stop traffic. As Leeds was the boundary between the West Yorkshire and Yorkshire WD areas, it was argued that the provision of staff to supervise traffic operating southbound from Leeds was Yorkshire WD's responsibility. The latter company was slow to make more than a vague offer of help, being itself very short of supervisory staff. An inspector was provided throughout the 1953 season but in 1954 the topic was again a matter of contention.

In 1952 an application was lodged to operate a night service between Newcastle and Liverpool FSu. Journeys would have departed southward at 10.30pm and northward 10.45pm, but the application was withdrawn in February 1953.

For 1953, the condition to operate duplicates from 6.00am onwards out of Leeds on summer Saturdays, was extended to services going to Manchester. The previous year BET chairmen had instructed their general managers to look into through bookings or linking of services to offer extra facilities to passengers. By December 1953 North Western and others were able to confirm that the following had been operated during the summer months, involving the Pool services:-

Barnsley - Manchester - Liverpool,
through vehicles daily
Newcastle - Manchester - North Wales,
through vehicles SO
Derby and Nottingham - Manchester -
Liverpool, daily throughout the year.

Other members of the Pool were carrying out similar exercises. A summer through service FSSu between Leeds and Edinburgh via Newcastle was operated in conjunction with Scottish Omnibuses, who were already long established as joint operators with United on three different Newcastle - Edinburgh services. Another United through booking in summer was Middlesbrough to Lowestoft via Leeds daily, with through coaches on Saturdays. This involved the Eastern Counties company.

The coach seated version offered a much better prospect, and is seen here in the form of Northern's **1724** (**FCN724**), a 1956 AEC. It was photographed outside the North Western depot at Hulme Hall Road, Manchester, with the overhead gantries of the Manchester, South Junction and Altrincham railway visible in the background. The line is now served by the trams of the Metrolink system. *(Photobus)*

West Yorkshire's last half-cab single deckers were delivered in 1952 and had 39 bus seats. When the change to the underfloor engined version came in 1953, it was accompanied by the specification of coach seating. The many Bristol LS and MW service coaches supplied in 1953-62 became stalwarts of the Limited Stop and played an important role in improving passenger comfort on the service. The company did not take delivery of the 45-seat bus version until 1963. At Darlington in August 1960 **EUG76** (**YWT290**) in the original red livery was photographed on its way to Newcastle. *(R A Stone)*

The earliest departure from Leeds to North Wales was at 10.25. It involved changing at Manchester with an hour's break, and arriving in Llandudno at 5.45pm. Passengers were requesting an earlier departure, to enable them to arrive at their hotels by lunch time instead of early evening. The Pool used the early duplication grant from Leeds in a way which, although 'legal until proved otherwise', was not as the Traffic Commissioners intended. A duplicate timing was introduced at 6.30am on Saturdays from Leeds, arriving in Manchester at 8.42. North Western left Manchester at 8.45 for North Wales, returning from Llandudno at 2.15pm. As neither licence had any duplication restriction on it, up to twenty vehicles could be seen on Saturday mornings at Leeds bound for North Wales.

There is no doubt that these extra facilities increased the Pool's income, and duplication was very heavy during the summer of 1954. On Saturday 31st July a total of 229 vehicles were operated. Only three companies, West Yorkshire, Yorkshire WD and North Western, found it necessary to hire vehicles to cover duplication, and a large percentage of these were used on the Leeds - Manchester section of the North Wales facility.

However Lancashire United complained about the additional mileage operated over their allocation and by the end of 1954 would only operate its own 11.7%.

28. 1956-57 - The Suez Crisis and After

In 1956 there was a further change of picking up point in Liverpool, from Russell Street to Canning Place, where LUT had an office. A new application for a night service was prepared but was held back for the moment. There were other problems. The Suez crisis meant reductions in services to save fuel. However it was decided to continue the existing timetable until after the Christmas period before reducing the service. The emergency service commenced on Sunday 30th December 1956, with a drastically cut timetable.

The emergency timetable consisted of two through services from Liverpool to Newcastle and return, with an additional timing from Newcastle to Manchester at 2.30pm on Saturdays. There were eleven return timings between Liverpool and Manchester as against fifteen previously, and seven between Manchester and Leeds as against fourteen. The service via Bradford was withdrawn.

A.T.Evans, the General Manager of United, was concerned about the local traffic carried on the Leeds - Middlesbrough service, which was licensed as stage carriage. Little change was made to this portion of the Pool.

By March 1957 the fuel rationing had finished and now was the time to restore the Pool to its previous running. This did not suit the companies, who considered it the time to make cuts. Their proposed timetable was divided into three. The winter timetable was to be the current emergency one, which would also be maintained TuWTh during the summer. The authorised existing summer timetable would operate FSSuM only. The Leeds - Middlesbrough service would be examined by United in view of the stage carriage operation. So began what would seem to many to be the decline of the Pool. Nevertheless, the service via Bradford was reinstated at Whitsun 1957 and operated FSSuM. In the following year, the long awaited Liverpool - Newcastle night service was introduced in May. It operated FSu throughout the summer period.

29. 1958-61 - The North Wales Imbroglio

In 1958 Wallace Arnold Tours of Leeds made applications for two express services, Leeds-Llandudno and Knottingley-Llandudno. These were objected to by the Pool, and the applications were refused. Wallace Arnold then appealed, but it was refused by the Minister. When later in the year the Pool's licences came up for renewal, Wallace Arnold objected on the grounds that through journeys between Yorkshire and North Wales were being advertised and operated. At the hearing on 19th January 1959 the North Western TC granted the renewal of the two licences not affected by the linking arrangements, but reserved his decision on the third until he had consulted with his opposite number in Yorkshire TA. Correspondence was received from the Traffic Commissioners reminding the Pool that the Minister had in the past indicated that in his view applicants should disclose their intention to link services. The Pool, after due consideration of the Commissioners' views, requested an amendment to the renewal application as follows:-

"To introduce a specific departure (to be indicated upon the timetables) at 6.30am from Leeds (Wellington Street Omnibus Station) to arrive Manchester (Lower Mosley Street Omnibus Station) at 8.42am on Saturdays only

Another coach type much used on the Limited Stop was the Harrington Cavalier, and this scene typifies the Pool workings of the 1960s. Yorkshire WD **763** (**BHD703**), an AEC, was hurrying through characteristic territory bound for Leeds. *(Photobus)*

Particularly distinctive were the 1954 Weymann-bodied Guy Arabs of Lancashire United. In pristine condition, **518** (**STF203**) was seen leaving Leeds (Wellington Street) for Liverpool, with a Ribble half-canopy coach in the background, loading for Blackpool. *(Jim Saunders)*

during the period of the summer timetable, viz from the Saturday before Whit Monday until the Saturday before the last Sunday in September. It is intended that after arrival at Manchester (Lower Mosley Street) vehicles operated from Leeds on the aforesaid timings shall (if traffic circumstances require it) proceed immediately to Llandudno and intermediate points on hire to North Western Road Car Co Ltd as duplicate vehicles upon the 8.45am departure to Llandudno authorised to that company by a road service licence the reference of which is CN1/341."

When the amendment was published in Notices & Proceedings both Wallace Arnold and Hanson objected to the condition. At the same time Wallace Arnold reapplied for a licence between Leeds and Llandudno. A joint hearing was held by the North Western and Yorkshire TC at Sheffield on 9th and 10th June 1959. A reserved decision was again given. On 15th October 1959 they gave a written reply granting the licence and the amendment, but were considering adding a further condition preventing the advertising of through facilities to North Wales on any other journeys. When the decision was printed in November 1959 the following had been added to the licence : "Save in respect of the journeys which are authorised to leave Leeds at 6.30am on certain Saturdays the holder of the licence shall not advertise or cause to be advertised the provision of through journeys to North Wales any portion of which is operated under the authority of the licence."

This led to further appeals. Wallace Arnold and Hanson opposed the grant to the Pool, and Wallace Arnold also appealed against the refusal of their Leeds-Llandudno service. The Pool appealed against the no advertising condition. It was some 20 months later on 16th August 1961 that the Minister gave his decision and removed the no advertising condition. In the period which followed, timetables showed the 'connecting' service to Llandudno from Newcastle as well as from Leeds. A Middlesbrough and Stockton link was made by clumsy stage carriage connections at Darlington, recalling Easton's arrangements of thirty years before. A small adjustment to allow a brief stop at Leeds would have allowed passengers to save an hour by travelling direct over the Middlesbrough-Leeds section.

30. Other Events of 1958-62

While this had been going on other things had been happening. It had been decided to wind up the Fawdon company, and the companies comprising the Limited Stop Pool and the Yorkshire Services Pool applied for the licences to operate the Newcastle to Coventry service. In the Northern TA the application was granted on 5th November 1958 to Northern, United, West Yorkshire, Yorkshire WD, North Western, Lancashire United, Yorkshire Traction, East Yorkshire and East Midland. The licence previously granted to the Fawdon Bus Co Ltd (TAR227/1) was surrendered. In the Yorkshire TA, the licences to West Yorkshire and the other companies were issued on 26th December 1958, a Friday. (Were they keen, or frantically late?!) The Fawdon company was placed in liquidation, and its final meeting took place on 4th July 1960. The Fawdon name disappeared, and timetables then usually advertised the service as the "Ten Cities Express". As Derby did not become a city until a later date, it was only possible to count nine at this time! These were Newcastle, Durham, Ripon, Leeds, Wakefield, Sheffield, Lichfield, Birmingham and Coventry. Timetable presentation was not consistent. West Yorkshire described the service as operated by "Yorkshire Services" and omitted reference to the other partners who were not members of the Yorkshire Services Pool. East Yorkshire ignored the Leeds-Newcastle section altogether. Northern's description was simply that it was operated by Northern and Yorkshire WD, which was the nearest description to the daily reality, both before and after the demise of the Fawdon company.

Although it had been agreed in 1956 that the "Automaticket" ticket machine should be used on the Pool services by all the operators, the Speed Setright was rapidly gaining in general popularity. In December 1957 a sub-committee was established to consider its possible use. It was not until February 1959 that the first order for Setright ticket rolls was placed, and even then Lancashire United remained outside the scheme and unwilling to adopt this system. A special pink ticket was introduced headed "Limited Stop Services" with all the names of the operators printed on the back.

The licences held by North Western and Lancashire United for a Manchester - Liverpool summer service SSuBH were surrendered in November 1959.

Another matter which involved lengthy correspondence was the introduction of route numbers. Their use was agreed in principle in December 1957, but it was not until the summer

An equally striking impression was created by a large group of Park Royal-bodied AECs new to Yorkshire WD in 1959. In this June scene that year at Manchester, Lower Mosley Street, **813** (**DHD193**) offered comprehensive destination detail including Eccles. The alternative routes via Eccles and Altrincham were rarely indicated on the vehicles themselves, but the need to ask which way the coach was going was removed the following summer when service numbers were introduced. *(G H F Atkins)*

This 1955 Roe-bodied Atkinson pictured at Leeds was another highly individualistic coach in the Lancashire United fleet. Note the external cab door and the company's distinctive red rose emblem. The use of the letters 'LUT' in the service number box indicates that this view of **558** (**WTB67**), bound for Middlesbrough, was taken before the 1960 introduction of numbers for the Pool services. Paper labels indicating "Leeds" and "Manchester" completed the information being offered to passengers. *(H W Peers)*

of 1960 that the following route numbers were introduced:-

X97 Liverpool - Newcastle via Altrincham
X98 Liverpool - Newcastle via Bradford
X99 Liverpool - Middlesbrough via Eccles.

They appeared in the subsequent winter timetables At first, United vehicles did not have 'X' on the blinds, and made do with '99' or '97' instead.

As ever, the operators were always alert to the competition. In this period the Pool noted with "grave concern" the proposals by British Railways to introduce a diesel service between Leeds and Liverpool on an hourly frequency.

31. 1962-63 - Speeding Up

Application was made in April 1962 to revise the X98 (ex-Tyne & Mersey) service by reducing the picking up points and speeding up the journey. After an amended timetable had been submitted, the application was granted in November 1962. The revised service omitted Bradford and cut an hour off the journey between Newcastle and Liverpool, operating one return journey daily in the summer season instead of FSSuM. There were only seven intermediate stopping places, which were Durham, Darlington, Harrogate, Leeds, Huddersfield, Oldham and Manchester. The route took the A580 East Lancashire Road between Liverpool and Manchester, the A62 main road between Huddersfield and Leeds, and the A1 by-passes at Catterick and Chester-le-Street. By contrast, the X97 had 21 intermediate stops plus 77 request stops. British Railways had objected to the proposals, contending that the whole purpose of reducing stops and speeding up the service was to attract a greater number of passengers. This would cause abstraction from rail services. They therefore appealed against the Commissioners' decision. The Minister upheld the appeal by attaching a condition to the Pool's vehicle allowance. This restricted the number of seats available as nearly as possible to the number of through passengers carried during the corresponding period of 1961. Through passengers were defined as those travelling from points between Newcastle and Harrogate inclusive to points between Dewsbury and Liverpool inclusive. Such a definition must have applied to the combined X97 and X98 services, because the X98 did not go through Dewsbury, and no doubt an equivalent point was used for defining through passengers via Bradford. Also included would be through passengers travelling on the X99 over the common section between Ripon and Liverpool. The calculation produced the restriction that duplication on the speeded up X98 should not exceed 16 vehicles in each direction on any one day or 188 duplicates in total in each direction during the season. As the period of operation was from the Friday before Whit Monday until the last Saturday in September, the number of days varied each year, but it was approximately 125. The duplication allowance therefore averaged only between one and two vehicles per day. To control the situation, advance booking was introduced as a necessity for the first time in the Pool's history.

"Cobbett", who was a retired Traffic Commissioner Chairman writing in "Bus and Coach" at that time, was surprised that it had taken the Pool so long to try and bring the service back to its pre-Suez level, since he realised that there were commercial advantages to be obtained in doing so. He further stated that British Railways had won a notable victory by persuading the Minister of Transport to limit the number of passengers which could be carried. He had thought that events were moving away from a rigid control on daily express services. It had seemed that the operators and Commissioners had made the Minister realise that if a service running daily throughout the year was to be any real help to the public at large, then there must be a complete flexibility regarding the number of people to be carried on any journey or day. He was not happy to see a service where pre-booking was at one time unnecessary now converted to a situation where pre-booking was essential. "Cobbett" even went further by advising operators to refute railway arguments about hypothetical abstraction of traffic and to make them prove it. He could see restrictions being imposed which would simply prevent people from travelling.

In the same period, several minor route changes were made as a result of severe traffic congestion or of new road construction. These were to and from the bus stations in Harrogate and Newcastle, and over the new Leeming by-pass, all announced to commence on 2nd March 1963. The Newcastle scheme involved northbound buses crossing the Tyne by the High Level bridge (instead of the Tyne bridge) to run direct to Haymarket bus station, and then turning south to terminate at Worswick Street. In the event this arrangement was not fully

The Limited Stop terminus in Liverpool was at Canning Place from 1956 to 1974, near the LUT office. It was much more central than the previous terminus in Russell Street. In this view dating from the early 1960s, Lancashire United **521** (**STF206**) had arrived at Canning Place on the X99, i.e. via Eccles. *(R H G Simpson)*

Another Lancashire United bus photographed after the introduction of service numbers was **435** (**MTB61**). This 1950 Guy Arab with Northern Counties body was heavy and solid and gave a good ride. It was leaving Manchester, Lower Mosley Street, on an X97 run to Liverpool via Altrincham. *(Jim Saunders Collection)*

implemented until the following year. In Northallerton, the SSu hospital journeys from Middlesbrough were cut back to the bus station in 1963. The overloading problems of 1952 had obviously evaporated. Indeed, these special journeys were withdrawn altogether in 1965 due to lack of demand. Also in 1965, arrangements were made, subject to a guarantee, to operate special vehicles for Airway Holidays from Leeds to Newcastle Airport. The Middlesbrough - Liverpool service was split operationally, with all passengers having to change at Leeds.

32. 1966 - Tyneside to the Potteries

Passengers from the Potteries wishing to travel to the north-east had had to use the Potteries Motor Traction X2 Newcastle-under-Lyme and Hanley service to Manchester, and change there to the Pool services. It was decided in 1966 to make application for a direct service on Friday nights and Sunday, operating from Hanley via Buxton and Barnsley to Newcastle. On other days it was still possible to travel on the X2 via Manchester as before, and at certain times this route was remarkably little slower than the new one. The direct service was numbered X95, was licensed to the six Pool partners and Potteries Motor Traction, and was timed at Leeds for crew changeovers. The Newcastle - Barnsley mileage was allocated to the Limited Stop Pool. The Barnsley - Hanley section was shared by North Western and Potteries, who operated 50% of the mileage each. Berresford's of Cheddleton near Leek, who objected on principle to any express operation out of the Potteries, also applied for a licence and were granted a limited one.

33. 1966 - New Brighton

In June 1966 an application was made to extend the X98 service to New Brighton on Saturdays. There was strong objection from British Railways. Evidence was given that since the revised X98 began operating in 1963 a substantial traffic for New Brighton had been cultivated from the north, and in 1965 some 700 passengers whose destination was New Brighton had made use of the service. The terminal point in Liverpool was a quarter of a mile from the underground railway station at James Street which provided a New Brighton service. Granting the application, the Traffic Commissioners stated that when passengers had

been on a coach for a matter of seven hours it was unreasonable to set them down in Liverpool to make their own way to New Brighton. This was the first direct service to the resort from any part of the country. The service commenced on 26th May 1967. On the same date the night service was transferred from the X97 to the X98 licence. With its adjusted timings, and having fewer stopping places than the X97, the revised X98 became one man operated at this time.

34. 1967 - New Services from Liverpool

Further services were introduced in May 1967. A direct service between Liverpool and Nottingham on Saturdays was numbered X92 and travelled via Warrington, Macclesfield and Derby. The X37 was from Liverpool to Skegness via Widnes and Warrington. Both services were operated by Lancashire United, North Western and Trent Motor Traction. The X37 also had Crosville as an operator. On both services the only way passengers could travel previously had been by the Pool to Manchester, changing there to the North Western and Trent services. In 1968 the Skegness service was extended to include Knutsford, Macclesfield and Buxton as picking up points.

With the speeding up of the X98 in 1963 Bradford, which had been served since 1928, had been removed as a picking up point, as mentioned in section 34 above. In 1968 application was made to extend one Leeds-Newcastle timing on Saturdays only to commence from Bradford at 9.05am, returning from Newcastle at 1.55pm. This operated summer only.

35. 1969-73 - The National Bus Company

The sale of British Electric Traction's bus interests to the Transport Holding Company in 1968 led to the formation of the National Bus Company on 1st January 1969. This brought the erstwhile BET and Tilling companies under one umbrella. The biggest change in the Pool services took place on 19th April 1970. The X98 was to operate twice daily throughout the year, but the night service only on Fridays for about seven weeks in July and August. The other through services were withdrawn, and uneven services were operated on the Liverpool - Leeds and Leeds - Newcastle sections. The Leeds - Middlesbrough section was separated from the other workings, and no longer provided convenient connections at Leeds to

Durham District Services Ltd of Darlington was owned by the British Transport Commission and managed by United but was not licensed to operate the Tyne - Tees - Mersey services. However, at busy times United would borrow its green vehicles and affix labels stating "On Hire to United". These two DDS pictures were taken in Wellington Street, Leeds. In the upper view **DU45 (SHN735)** was just about to enter the coach station on a "97" duplicate from Darlington in the period 1965-67. **DBE34 (7434HN)**, in the period 1962-64 *(below)*, had coach seating and was much more suitable for this service. It was being prepared for the return trip to Darlington. After the numbering of the Pool routes in 1960, United gradually added "X" to the number blinds in its fleet, but DDS did not have any services with an "X" prefix and so continued to make do with "97" for these journeys. *(R F Mack Collection; Ribble Enthusiasts)*

and from Liverpool. All reservations on the X98 had to be booked 48 hours in advance. It was rather ironical that the ex-Tyne & Mersey licence was to be the only through service coast to coast, and that it was once again publicised as the Tyne & Mersey service.

In 1970 the Yorkshire WD interest in the Pool was transferred to Hebble Motor Services who then became an operator. In the Northern TA, for example, the Hebble applications were granted on 16th September 1970 and the Yorkshire WD licences surrendered. At the end of the year, North Western withdrew its 160 Oldham-Huddersfield service on 30th December.

In the summer of 1971, Hebble moved from its long established address at Walnut Street, Halifax, to Frost Hill, Liversedge, and again to Belle Isle, Wakefield. A similar process affected North Western a little later, with the head office moving from Charles Street, Stockport, to the company's Wilmslow office early in 1972, and again to the Ribble headquarters at Frenchwood Avenue, Preston, on 1st September. Ribble was now responsible for North Western's operations.

By 1972, when the major part of the M62 motorway had opened, the X98 operated direct between Manchester and Huddersfield. The X97 and X99 between Manchester and Leeds still operated via Oldham and Mirfield. The bus station at Lower Mosley Street, Manchester, a vital element in the operation of the Limited Stop for 44 years, closed on 13th May 1973. The Pool services were transferred to Chorlton Street bus station, not far from Piccadilly, and North Western's head office transferred there from Preston in the autumn.

36. 1973-75 - From Limited Stop to National Express

For over four years from 1st January 1969, the majority of express services throughout England and Wales had been operated by firms which were owned by the National Bus Company. From this situation came a new concept for express services, under the aegis of the Central Activities Group which was to control coaching and travel developments. The first step was the establishing of a company called National Travel (NBC) Ltd, which was actually London Coastal Coaches Ltd renamed. This company was to coordinate and market the express services under the corporate image of the white coach. Five area managers were appointed, and from 1st October 1973 most express services were presented under the name "National" with the actual operator's own name shown in much smaller lettering. The individual companies were running the services on behalf of National Travel (NBC) Ltd. By April 1974 the five areas had been made into five separate companies, two of which were partners in the Limited Stop Pool. For this new role, Hebble had been renamed National Travel (North East) Ltd on 24th January 1974, and North Western became National Travel (North West) Ltd on 6th February. Thus, when an application was made in February 1973 for a direct service between Leeds and Llandudno avoiding Manchester, it was for operation on summer Saturdays by Hebble, Lancashire United, North Western, Northern, United and West Yorkshire. When the licences were eventually granted a year later they were to National Travel (North East) in place of Hebble and National Travel (North West) in place of North Western, the others remaining the same.

At the same time, an application was made by Northern and Crosville for a direct service betwen Newcastle and Pwllheli via Rhyl and Llandudno. Both this and the Leeds - Llandudno service were intended to replace the linked facilities through Manchester. The Pwllheli service operated on summer Saturdays with a crew changeover at Knutsford service station on the M6, and was granted for the 1973 season. The service from Leeds had to persist with the linked arrangements via Manchester in 1973, with the delay in licensing being possibly due to objections in the Yorkshire TA. It was noticeable that North Western were not involved in the Pwllheli service. In similar vein, an application was made by United for a special

NORTH WESTERN
&
JOINT OPERATORS

All express services will arrive & depart from this station from Monday 14 May '73

From this date Lower Mosley St. station will be closed.

A journey on the speeded-up Pool service X98 was being worked by United's **UE702** (**902THN**) when this picture was taken in Wellington Street, Leeds, in July 1968. The coach was in the olive green livery associated with, but not inherited from, Orange Bros Ltd, formerly of Bedlington, Northumberland. *(PB Collection)*

Thirty-six-feet long vehicles had been introduced in 1962 but it was several years before such coaches were regularly operating the Tyne - Tees - Mersey services. In the last few years of the Pool's existence, coaches like North Western's **143** (**AJA143B**) with stylish Alexander body were in use, often with revised liveries. This was the scene at Leeds on 31st October 1971. *(Gerald Knox)*

student service to operate from Durham to Manchester and Liverpool. Previously, all these would have been Pool joint licence applications, the last of which was made in October 1973 for a service between Wakefield and Manchester. The change could be seen as the 'writing on the wall' for the very existence of the Limited Stop Pool.

The Pool services came under the control of National Travel (North East) and in April 1974 the services were renumbered into the National Express network. The X97-X99 Liverpool services became 397-399, the X95 Hanley service 395, and Coventry 313/314. The Liverpool-Middlesbrough licence was surrendered, and the Leeds-Middlesbrough section replaced by a joint United and West Yorkshire X99 service. This resurrected the situation of forty years before, prior to United's full membership of the Pool.

Because of LUT's involvement in the Pool, it was still necessary to operate according to the original mileage agreements. This was to change very shortly when a large scheme involving Ribble, Crosville, Lancashire United and the Merseyside and Greater Manchester PTEs took effect. Accordingly, on 27th April 1974 Ribble took over LUT's mileage entitlement, not only on the Pool services (including Leeds - Llandudno and Hanley - Newcastle) but also those from Liverpool to Nottingham and to Skegness. This new situation enabled National Travel to use vehicles to best advantage, as companies were paid per mile operated rather than on a revenue sharing basis. The revenue was paid direct to National Travel. Services were run under the banner of the National express network, with the emphasis on the word "National". It was not until coaching deregulation under the 1980 Act that coaches began to carry the brand name "National Express", although the name had appeared on timetables from 1974.

For passengers paying on the bus, Ribble crews were instructed to issue Setright express single or return tickets "in the normal manner", i.e. Ribble company tickets rather than the pink ones headed "Limited Stop Services". Another change that coincided with the transfer from LUT to Ribble on 27th April 1974 was a further move of the Pool services' Liverpool terminus, from the LUT office in Canning Place to Mann Island, Pier Head. The original intention was to move it to South John Street, and agents were actually notified that such a move would take

effect on 25th May, but in the event the proposals were short-circuited by the new Ribble arrangements. An odd twist to the new terminus was that supervision of the service was done not by Ribble inspectors but by Crosville's. Indeed, Crosville also carried out supervision at Warrington on behalf of the Pool.

On 4th May 1975 the now-separate X99 Leeds - Middlesbrough service was extended north to Hartlepool and Sunderland and numbered 399 as a National Express service. It was nevertheless on a stage-carriage licence and the operators remained as United and West Yorkshire. Later in 1975 the individual names of companies operating the Limited Stop service disappeared from the timetables. The last one issued in October 1975 showed Northern, United, West Yorkshire, Ribble, National Travel (North East) and National Travel (North West). The licences were now being held by National Travel (North East), and the Pool arrangements were no longer necessary or in force. In this quiet way the Limited Stop Pool, which had operated such intensive long distance services in the north of England for 45 years, just faded away almost unnoticed.

37. 1986 - Tailpiece

After fifty years of strict control, fresh independent opportunities were heralded by the Transport Acts of 1980 and 1985. The days of the Limited Stop were recalled in 1986 when "Travelux" commenced a daily service from Teesside to Leeds on 3rd March. The proprietor was Terry Barvir of Nunthorpe near Middlesbrough, who ran the service virtually single handed. This meant driving to Leeds and back once on Sundays and twice every other day, although he must have had help in order to take the statutory rest periods. Not only did he advertise the service as "The X99 Leeds Link" and show the number X99 on the coach, but his route also reflected some of the history of the Limited Stop. Commencing at Billingham, he ran via Stockton to Middlesbrough and thence via Stokesley, Osmotherley and Northallerton. With some originality he operated via the A167, A1, A58 and A659 to Harewood House, by-passing Thirsk, Boroughbridge and Wetherby and then entering Leeds via Headingley to serve the University. It was not to last. Terry Barvir died suddenly in November 1986, and the service ceased with him. Perhaps he had tried too hard.

By 1974 the liveries of the National Bus Company had been applied to vehicles operating the Limited Stop. Here on 15th April West Yorkshire's **1068** (**8125WX**) in the local coach colours had arrived at the recently rebuilt version of the Haymarket bus station in Newcastle. *(Philip Battersby)*

On 27th April 1974 the Liverpool terminus was transferred from Canning Place to Mann Island, Pier Head. On 3rd October 1975 North Western's **241** (**JDB241E**) had arrived there from Manchester via Altrincham on the 397 and was ready to return the same way. By this time the universal white livery of National Travel had swallowed up those of all the constituent companies, the North Western name was already an anachronism, and the Pool arrangements between the companies had been superseded by the new regime. Thus did the Pool come to an end, and so likewise does this book. *(Philip Battersby)*